NURSE GEORGEE

AN ACCOUNT OF MY JOURNEY THROUGH NURSING AND HOW GOD LED ME TO BE A WITNESS FOR HIM

Georgia Cohen

PRESS

KIND THOUGHTS
FROM FRIENDS

I was blessed to have taken an evangelism class that Pastor Georgia taught. I feel her willingness to teach and to share the Gospel is amazing. I have been involved with other evangelism classes taught by very well-known pastors and none are any better than Pastor Georgia. Her bold willingness to share God's greatest gift with others in any situation has helped me to gain the confidence to share as well. Her passion for the Gospel is contagious! I pray all will become infected with her passion for the Gospel.
Tom Boyle Cornerstone Insurance Solutions Pittsburgh, Pennsylvania

Nurse Georgia makes you feel like you've been best friends forever. Her stories draw you in because they are so relatable in their humanness. With humor, she shares her life lessons of genuine humility and gut wrenching honesty while pursuing God with unashamed love. Georgia's gift of encouragement draws your focus to God, His love, and His word and gives you the confidence to help others do the same.
Janet Howard Owner of Oh My Yum Bakery Herriman, Utah

Georgia has a heart that is on fire for Jesus. And, surely enough, this fire will lighten up your soul as soon as you hear her testimony. During her METS presentation, one of the most memorable stories was when she had to overcome her shyness and practically scream into the ears of a nearly deaf patient the words of a salvation prayer in front of other medical workers. That boldness for God that Georgia has is outstanding. I think it is one of the most important qualities that are missing in so many Christians today. To be bold for Jesus; that's what I learned from this beautiful, godly woman.

Vera Lyubasyuk 3rd year medical student at University of California, San Diego School of Medicine

I am a registered nurse and worked with Georgia in the Coronary Care Unit. What a rewarding experience it became, however it certainly did not start out that way. Those first few months were pure torture. As God began to work His powers in the CCU, we saw our prayers answered right before our eyes. It was a joy to see patients and family members become children of God. Georgia was able to reach out to others in such a profound way. She has a bold, loving, and caring spirit that is such a part of who she is and the life that she lives.

Carole McWilliams RN Germantown, Maryland
Clinical Supervisor of Cardiac Cath Lab and Heart Station at George Washington University Hospital

Georgia has had a life of rich experiences in the Lord and I'm so glad she has written this book in order to share some of them with us. I lead a long standing weekly prayer group and one of our favorite speakers has always been Georgia. Her enthusiasm for God is contagious and she will motivate and inspire you to fulfill your God given destiny. As Georgia shares, her wonderful sense of humor combined with deep spiritual truths will keep your interest from beginning to end. Georgia and I served on the board of Hospital Christian Fellowship for many years. Georgia is a woman who is passionate about Jesus Christ and is a woman of integrity and honor.

Carol Nomides RN Pittsburgh, Pennsylvania

Georgia's impact for Christ exceeds what I thought possible in a health care environment. Her stories consistently inspire me

to pray for divine appointments in the workplace and, indeed, to seize the moment when they come.
Jessie Paul RN Toronto, Canada

Georgia Cohen is an anointed, vibrant, life giving woman. Georgia is full of faith and, like the "energizer bunny," she is constantly finding the "unsaved" to bring them the gospel. I pray that each person that reads this book would catch Georgia's fiery, joyful, spiritual life. Actually, this book can be used to stir up any waning ministry. Georgia is used in hospitals, churches, Aglow meetings, and everywhere she is called. It's been said, "There are no rocking chairs in God's Kingdom." Look out, here comes Georgia, to bring Jesus, salvation, healing, and deliverance. "Enjoy!"
Rev. Evelyn Steele Founding President North Eastern U.S. Aglow/ National Director, Aglow Int'l

CONTENTS

Preface.. xiii

Chapter 1 How Do I Share the Good News
              with My Patients? 15

Chapter 2 I Was the Best Silent Witness 22

Chapter 3 City of Faith Hospital or Pit of Hell............28

Chapter 4 Love Your Enemies – Really?....................38

Chapter 5 My First Prayer in CCU 49

Chapter 6 Be Still and Listen (Chuck and Anna)........54

Chapter 7 Two Steps Forward, Three Steps Back 60

Chapter 8 Enter Joe – Another Chance 65

Chapter 9 Big John – I Saw Jesus 71

Chapter 10 Meet Our 94-Year-Old-Jewish Lady.........76

Chapter 11 Poppy – My Jewish Father-In-Law............81

Chapter 12 Policeman and Neighbor Pete 85

Chapter 13 Max (AKA Mr. Elephant)...........................88

Chapter 14 NO! NO! I've Seen Too Much 93

Chapter 15 Eyes Like Diamonds.................................96

Chapter 16 I Want to Donate My Organs 99

Chapter 17 Hell's Angels Versus the Outlaws 105

Chapter 18 I'm a Catholic 109

Chapter 19 Grandma's Cross 115

Chapter 20 Big Mac Attacks.....................................120

Chapter 21 I'm an Episcopalian 124

Chapter 22 He's in My Heart 128

Chapter 23 Look for the Spiritual Diagnosis 131

Chapter 24 The Bottom Line..134
Chapter 25 Witnessing Tips..136
Chapter 26 **YOU CAN DO IT!** 140

ACKNOWLEDGEMENTS

Barbara Osinski, my only sister, has blessed my ministries with her continual giving of offerings throughout my life of serving. Thank you, Barb, for your faithfulness. God has used you to promote the gospel of Jesus Christ. Thank you for all you have done for the Kingdom of GOD.

My precious son **Scott** and precious daughter **Colette Lord** were remarkably phenomenal with their line editing. Their focus on sentence restructuring throughout the entire manuscript; twice, helped to improve the overall flow of this book. Thank you for your constant encouragement. I never would have been able to complete this task without you. Colette, when you told me that you hear me talking when you read the stories, I was reassured that I accomplished the purpose of my writing.

Ginger Fuller, my precious daughter. I thank you for reviewing excerpts of my manuscript. Your insights were valuable to me and appreciated.

Jill Furniss did a fantastic job with basic copyediting. Thank you for the time you spent editing while trying to maintain a busy household and caring for a very sick pet.

Kate Gallogly, my great niece, encouraged me with her drawings. Never give up honey. You have a great talent and God wants to use you.

Holly Gallogly's teaching experience helped me to collect my thoughts and express them coherently. Holly, you taught me how to write, drawing the details of my experiences from my inner most being. You got me off to a good start. Thank you for the time you spent with me.

Last but certainly not least is my dear husband **Bill.** Thank you, honey, for helping me to restrain myself when I was ready to smash my computer into little bitty pieces. You were patient with me while teaching me how to use my computer. I love you dearly. Your Tiger! XOXOXOXOXO

PREFACE

The year was 1973. The date: October 2nd. It was a crisp, autumn Tuesday morning. Looking out my bedroom window, I couldn't help but notice the sun's rays reflecting off the golden maple leaves. Upon awaking, I had no idea that today would mark a pivotal moment in my life.

The time was 2:30 P.M. I had just put my youngest baby down for a nap. Overwhelmed with the desire to pray, I knelt beside my bed, folded my hands, and realized that I didn't know how to pray. Where do I even begin? Immediately, I remembered my sister Barbara telling me that I needed Jesus. The prayer that followed changed my life forever. *Jesus, why do I need You?* Supernaturally, my sins were laid before me. For the first time in my life, I realized that I was a sinner.

Jesus compassionately spoke and said, *Give your sins to Me. Georgia, this is why I came; to save you from yourself. I want to live My life through you. Will you accept Me as your Savior and Lord?*

"Yes," I responded immediately. Instantly, I was changed from a depressed young woman into a vibrant human being. Jesus washed me clean, as white as snow, when He covered my sins on the cross with His blood. The human race is stuck in pits of despair, depression, anxiety, and lack of self-worth, waiting to be delivered. Can such deliverance be found? Yes! Deliverance from sin is available to everyone. When we invite Jesus into our life, and ask Him to forgive us of our sins, it is a done deal. Not only

does He forgive us of our sins, but He also forgets our sins. Oh, what a Savior.

Once a caterpillar emerges from its cocoon as a colorful butterfly, it never again tries to crawl back into that cocoon. It will never be encased in a world of silence and darkness again. The butterfly replaces the isolation of its cocoon for freedom. When a person is transformed by the power of God, he is released from his cocoon and called to give the world a witness of his freedom from the kingdom of darkness to the kingdom of light.

When I was set free from my cocoon prison, the love of God radiated from every pore in my body. The excitement of knowing Jesus and having Him in my life was overwhelming. I couldn't wait to tell the world about my Savior and to let people know that they too could have peace everlasting.

Where and how would I even begin to tell others about Jesus? As a nurse, I longed to pray for my patients and peers. Over the years, through trial and error, Jesus has patiently taught me how to approach others.

If you have ever struggled with being a witness for God, then this book is for you. Be encouraged as you read how the Lord patiently held my hand, walking me through, step by step, in His school of obedience. The days of being a silent witness are over. The world needs peace and comfort. Let's be willing to come out of our cocoon and be the witness that God has called us to be.

This book is dedicated to my Lord and Savior, Jesus Christ. Without Him, I am nothing. I owe everything to Him. He alone is worthy. He deserves all the glory, all the honor, forever and ever. My prayer for you is that through reading this book, you will be encouraged to tell the world that JESUS IS ALIVE. His grave is empty!

CHAPTER 1
HOW DO I SHARE THE GOOD NEWS WITH MY PATIENTS?

Since 2:30 P.M. on October 2, 1973, I have never lost my desire to tell others that Jesus loves them and gave His life for them. However, for many years, I was still afraid to approach others. I was fearful of witnessing. I struggled with opening my mouth and offering prayer to my close encounters. The desire to do something, and acting on that desire, conflicted within me. My greatest desire was to tell my family and patients about my wonderful Savior. How would I even begin? The first thing I realized was that I needed to get my eyes off myself and onto Jesus. I had to admit that I was more concerned with the possible rejection from my peers, family, and friends than I was with offering Jesus to a broken, hopeless, human race.

Jesus' purpose was to seek and save the lost. Once I was lost and now I am found. Jesus found me and saved me from my sins. How could I keep quiet about what the Lord had done for me? Disobedience, fear of man, and rejection kept me in chains—silent witness chains. PURE SELFISHNESS! I was more concerned about what others thought of me than their eternal damnation.

Coming to grips with my selfishness was painful. When I realized that no one cared for me like Jesus, I made up my mind. I would open my mouth, stutter out a few words about Jesus to those who crossed my path, maybe fall flat on my face, get up, and try again. I would no longer be a silent witness. Regardless of how poor a presentation of the gospel I offered, I would not be silent.

Nurses training taught me how to provide physical care. Spiritual care, however, was never addressed. We are created with a spiritual nature along with our physical body. Why is it that the medical profession had totally neglected this significant part of our being? When the realization of the need for spiritual care became evident, I yearned to start addressing it.

The Joint Commission (TJC), formerly the Joint Commission on Accreditation of Healthcare Organizations (JCAHO), is the organization that accredits health care organizations in the United States. Now TJC requires hospitals to include a spiritual assessment as part of the overall assessment of a patient. On a patient's original history and physical assessment upon admission to a hospital, spiritual questions are to be asked of each patient. Every patient's care plan will have spiritual care addressed by the nurse.

Yes, yes, yes! A nurse can ethically give spiritual care to patients. Suggestions of questions a nurse or physician might ask according to TJC can be found at www.jointcommission.org/standards_information.

Nursing care reveals the spiritual hunger in patients. The hospital environment is foreign, sterile, beeping with machines, and blazing with florescent lights. Patients feel isolated, fearful, and uninformed. Upon entering each patient's room, I always found myself enveloped in an atmosphere of anxiety. My comforting words never seemed to dissipate the patient's fear. My words were useless. I realized there was only one way to dispel fear. The Bible tells us in 2 Timothy 1:7 (KJV): "For God hath not given us the spirit of fear; but of power, and of love and of a sound mind." The only way my patients would have peace would be to surrender their fears and concerns to God.

"For He [God] satisfieth the longing soul" [Psalm 107:9 (KJV)]. Only God can satisfy our longing soul. I was so excited to tell my patients about my wonderful discovery. Now they, too, could know that they were not alone. The Bible tells us in Hebrews 13:5b, that God said; "Never will I leave you, never will I forsake you." This is good news, and the world needs good news, especially the patient who is flat on his back in a hospital bed. My excitement was overwhelming. I couldn't wait to share this good news with my patients.

Where would I even start? How does one begin to tell others that Jesus loves them without appearing to offend their religion? Pondering this concern, I realized that I would not be criticizing someone's religion if I simply shared that Jesus loves them. It is not about a religion at all; it is about a relationship with Jesus, which transcends religion. This realization freed me and filled me with hope and excitement. I was joyful and elated to start sharing this good news with any anxious and fearful patient who might be interested.

Here we go again. This head knowledge still left me intimidated when approaching my patients about where they were spiritually in their relationship with Jesus. I was still scared, selfish, and afraid of rejection. I had no idea how to even start to discuss spiritual care with a patient. Again, I analyzed my fears. I had to admit that I was still concerned that I might offend someone's religion when I talked with them about Jesus. I was a Protestant. My city is predominately Catholic. My objective was not to promote my Protestant religion to others. Far from it! I just wanted everyone to experience the unspeakable joy that I now had in my relationship with Jesus. Meditating on my situation, I realized that I was offering a relationship with Jesus; I was not discussing religion.

The book of John describes a discussion between Jesus and a man named Nicodemus. Jesus told this Jewish man that he must be born-again. Nicodemus would be considered a scholar of scholars today. He was a Pharisee, one of the religious leaders of his time. Apparently, Nicodemus had been spying on Jesus and had some questions of his own. Approaching Jesus at night (hoping that he would not be seen by the other Pharisees), he questioned Jesus:

"How can someone be born (again) when they are old?" Nicodemus asked. "Surely they cannot enter a second time into their mother's womb to be born!"

Jesus answered, "Very truly I tell you, no one can enter the kingdom of God unless they are born of water and the Spirit. Flesh gives birth to flesh, but the Spirit gives birth to spirit. You should not be surprised at my saying, 'You must be born-again.'"

John 3:4-7

Jesus was not promoting a religion. Jesus was saying to Nicodemus, a Jewish man, that He wanted his spiritual nature to come alive, to be born-again, so they could have a relationship and communicate with each other.

The clouds of confusion were dissipating. I now understood. When I talked with someone about Jesus and His love for them, I was only talking about having a relationship with the King of kings and the Lord of lords. John 15:13 tells us, "Greater love has no one than this: to lay down one's life for one's friends." Jesus gave His life so we could live our life to the fullest, knowing that when we die, we will be forever with Him. Now that, my friend, is something to shout about!

However, all this head knowledge did little to calm my fears when it came to witnessing about Jesus and His love for us. I remained terrified when witnessing opportunities were presented to me. Seeking God in earnest concerning where to even begin to approach patients about their spiritual nature, I felt that God was reminding me of another time in my life when I was faced with a frightening situation. God helped me get through my probation period during nurse's training. He helped me then, and I knew He would help me now to master my fear of witnessing.

Probee Days Are Here Again

I was a student nurse and had to give my first shot. I was terrified. My clinical instructor, Mrs. Muttle, was overbearing. She reminded me of what an Army drill sergeant might be like. After finishing our theory on injections, it was time for the practicum. Our sergeant, Mrs. Muttle, was giving us last-minute orders on how to give an intramuscular injection as we huddled in a circle in the 3 S (3rd floor) nurse's station. "Betty," the sergeant's voice boomed, "You will be the first one to give the injection." Betty tried to remain calm as she drew up the penicillin. Soon, she was off to the battlefield with Sergeant Muttle leading the way. Within two minutes, the patient's door flung open as Betty ran out with tears streaming down her cheeks. Sergeant's mouth never stopped flapping. Her bellowing voice infiltrated the nursing unit. "How many times do I have to tell you to make sure that the needle is securely fastened to the hub of the syringe?" Betty was able to get the needle into the patient's buttock, but when she went to inject the penicillin, the needle broke from the syringe. Penicillin was sprayed over the patient's buttock and everywhere else. As Betty tried to regain her composure, Sergeant Muttle grabbed Ann as her next victim. Ann seemed calm enough as she drew up her medication. Sergeant Muttle waved her arms, pushing us aside as she led the way to the next battlefield. I thought I could actually hear her yelling, "hut two-three-four." Ann entered room 3034 and the patient's door closed ever so slowly, seeming to lock her in. We students stood in the nurse's station and breathed a sigh of relief as that door closed. Sweet relief that we were not the chosen ones this time! Too soon we heard Sergeant Muttle's harsh voice as door number 3034 flew open. Ann ran out of the room, still holding the syringe with the needle attached. The needle looked like the letter Z.

"How many times do I have to tell you how to give an intra-muscular injection?"

Through heaving sobs, Ann finally was able to speak. "I couldn't help it; his buttock was made of leather!"

Sergeant Muttle was furious. "Back to the classroom with you sorry lot; we will have two more weeks of theory and practice and then attempt this practicum again."

Sergeant's voice groaned on and on over the next two weeks of theory. I thought it would never end. I had nightmares of leather buttocks, covered in penicillin! It was soon to get worse. The first time Sergeant Muttle taught us how to give shots, we practiced on oranges. Things were different now. Sergeant decided that we would now practice on each other. Each day we practiced injecting each other in the thighs, buttocks, hips, and arms. Of course we didn't inject anything into each other. It was simply target practice and technique that were stressed. By the end of the two weeks, we students were hobbling around like little old ladies.

Finally, we were back in the nurse's station on 3 S. I quickly came to attention when I heard Sergeant Muttle call my name. "Georgia," her voice rumbled in my ears so loudly that it felt as if the whole nurse's station shook from an earthquake shock wave, "You will go first today."

I was instantly terrified. My hands shook as I drew up the medication in the syringe. I couldn't believe that my feet actually moved one in front of the other as we marched down the long hallway on 3 S. My mind raced with thoughts of Betty's and Ann's experiences. Did I make sure that the needle was tight enough on the syringe? Will I be able to get this needle into the patient's buttock? Walking down that long hallway, the nightmare of my patient's buttock being leather and covered in penicillin consumed my thoughts, instantly ramping up my anxiety and fear. Sweating, knees knocking, and heart racing, I questioned my ability to give this shot. The sound of the syringe and needle bouncing around on my metal medicine tray in my shaking hands was almost deafening. I felt like I was about to have a grand mal seizure. I looked down at the syringe and needle on the wavering tray and panicked. The syringe and needle had grown larger than the medicine tray I was carrying. I was caving in. "I can't do this," I thought, as I walked all the way to the end of the longest hallway to approach the patient's room. Each step brought me closer to doom and damnation. Each step marked the closing in of the end of my dream to be a nurse. Another glance at the syringe confirmed my fears. The needle loomed large and intimidating. It mocked me, and I took a deep breath. Moments before approaching the patient's room, which was the last room on the left side of the hallway, I said to myself, "If you want to be a nurse, you have to know how to give a shot. You can do this." Before I knew it, I was at the patient's bedside with the syringe in my hand. Guess what? I did it! I gave my first injection! I actually got the needle into the patient's buttock and injected the medication, with the needle remaining attached to the hub of the syringe. You know what? Since that time, years ago, I have given thousands of shots. I don't even think about it anymore. I just do it. You see, my friend, it is the same when it comes to telling someone about the love of Jesus. You just do it. The more you share with someone that Jesus loves them and has a plan for their life, the easier it gets. Just like giving a shot.

CHAPTER 2
I WAS THE BEST
SILENT WITNESS

The secret in witnessing to others about the love of Jesus is to just do it. Just like giving a shot. I get it. Yet, I struggled with taking my own advice after the realization and connection with giving my first shot. I seldom witnessed. I infrequently prayed with my patients. I knew what I wanted to do. I knew what Jesus wanted me to do. But still, there was a river to cross, and I didn't have a boat.

The first few months that followed my October born-again experience in 1973 were consumed with me telling others about Jesus. Why did I stop witnessing after that?

Early one morning during my time with the Lord, I began to reflect on my experience in October of 1973. I recalled how enthusiastic I was in telling my friends and loved ones that Jesus was now in my life. Yes! I remember telling everyone that they too could have and experience the love of Jesus. Countless times, I shared with anyone willing to listen that in my depths of depression and despair, I had called out to Jesus and said, "If You are for real and if I need You, would You show up?" I shared how Jesus in His tender mercy wrapped His loving arms around me and said He wanted to be Lord of my life. In total surrender, I told Him that it would be good to share my life with Him. I asked Him to forgive me of my sins and thanked Him for accepting me just as

I am. Immediately, I was saturated in the peace of God; peace that I have never known. I was changed. I was a new woman. The desire of my heart was for everyone I came in contact with to experience Jesus and have this eternal peace. Fast forward ten years later. Why did I stop witnessing? What happened to me? How and why did I become a silent witness?

Pondering the events over the past ten years, I realized that I had let the fear of man take control of the throne of my life. Fear of rejection now lived on that throne. My family was turned off by my "Good News." They were tired of hearing Jesus – Jesus – Jesus! I found myself pulling back from witnessing. I became a "silent witness."

Of course I wanted my family and friends to have and experience Jesus Christ; to know that they too can be free in Him, free from past guilt and sin. Unfortunately, I was clueless when it came to sharing my faith. I was zealous with a capital Z. My excitement was a little overwhelming to those I love. Every time I saw someone, even strangers, I talked about Jesus and the need to accept Him as their Savior. The only thing I accomplished was to distance my loved ones from my presence. Even my own mother said that Jesus was destroying our relationship. I couldn't believe it. This was the same mother that dragged me to church every Sunday. Wouldn't you think she would share my excitement? How could this be? For the first time in my life, I knew that I was loved and accepted, all because of Jesus. Yet, this new freedom in Christ was alienating me from my family and friends. It wasn't long before my friends and family made an immediate about-face and literally ran the other way when they saw me approaching. My family never came to visit anymore. The brick house finally caved in on me. Finding myself alone, never receiving phone calls or invitations to join others for lunch, I diagnosed the problem. It was my mouth and my excitement about my precious Savior. I developed a fear of sharing my faith. No one likes to be rejected. By keeping my mouth shut, I noticed that my family was slowly accepting me again. Thus, I became the "silent witness." The desire to be a witness for my precious Savior had been replaced by the spirit of fear. The fear of man dominated my every thought and move. It was about time that I admitted that I had become a strangled witness or, better yet, no witness at all.

Ten years. Ten years is a long time. Yep! I am so ashamed to admit that ten long, silent years had now come and gone since I came face to face with Jesus. I was the best "silent witness." I was a good nurse, taking my position seriously by genuinely caring about the welfare of my patients. I was compassionate and understanding. I convinced myself that the joy of the Lord would be so obvious in my countenance that my patients would ask me why I was so happy and peaceful. Then, I would be able to tell them that Jesus is the reason for my joy. This rationalization never fully opened the door to share what I had experienced concerning the love of Jesus. There were no excuses. How could I ever forget? I was totally transformed. I was set free from the lies and false accusations of my past. How could I have had a face-to-face experience with the creator of this universe and kept silent about His existence? It was time to confront my enemies: rejection and the fear of man. These two accusers kept me silent way too long.

During my daily time with the Lord, before going to work, I began visualizing myself dressed and ready for battle with the armor of God.

"Finally, be strong in the Lord and in his mighty power. Put on the full armor of God, so that you can take your stand against the devil's schemes. For our struggle is not against flesh and blood, but against the rulers, against the authorities, against the powers, of this dark world and against the spiritual forces of evil in the heavenly realms. Therefore put on the full armor of God, so that when the day of evil comes, you may be able to stand your ground, and after you have done everything, to stand. Stand firm then, with the belt of truth buckled around your waist, with the breastplate of righteousness in place, and with your feet fitted with the readiness that comes from the gospel of peace. In addition to all this, take up the shield of faith, with which you can extinguish all the flaming arrows of the evil one. Take the helmet of salvation and the sword of the Spirit, which is the word of God."

-Ephesians 6:10-17

Every day before work, I dressed myself in the full armor of God. Lead on, oh King Eternal. I am prepared for battle. I am prayed up and ready to go, so I thought. As soon as I came face-to-face with a patient, my desire to pray was overshadowed by intense fear. It was like a gradual snow storm that turned into a full-blown avalanche. My enemies of fear and doubt immobilized me. I found myself frozen in my own made-up avalanche. It was a long war. Two steps forward, three steps back. My armor had holes in it. The holes were my lack of trust in my Lord. The holes had to go and that was that. I purposed in my heart that above all else I would trust in the Lord and not in myself. He promises to direct and guide me. Refusing to give up, I stammered and stuttered when offering to pray with my patients. My feeble attempts at witnessing caused me to get serious about telling my world what Jesus had done for me. It was time to regroup and refocus. I needed some serious quiet time alone with the Lord. Yes, I needed a retreat with my God.

I went away for five days to Jumonville, a Methodist church camp in Pennsylvania. The camp was unoccupied during early spring. The seclusion was wonderful. I spent the time alone with my Bible, my thoughts, my prayers, and my precious Savior, while enjoying the pleasant grounds and fresh air. Sensing the presence of the Lord as I strolled through the woods, I gazed at the blue sky filled with white, puffy clouds. Longing to pray for my patients with no idea of where and how to really do this, I felt like a helpless child calling out to God.

Lord, I quietly whispered, as I walked through the wooded camp, *would You teach me how to tell others that You love them? Teach me how to pray and encourage my patients.*

The chill in the air led me back to the cabin. I built a fire and snuggled up with a blanket to watch the embers flicker in the fireplace. Opening my Bible, I started to read the book of Isaiah. Slowly sipping my hot coffee, I found myself caught up in the life of this Old Testament prophet. Turning the page to chapter six, I began to read:

> "In the year that King Uzziah died I saw also the Lord sitting upon a throne, high and lifted up and His train filled the temple.
> Above it stood the seraphim each one had six wings; with twain he covered his face, and with twain he covered his feet, and with twain he did fly.
> And one cried unto another, and said, Holy, Holy, Holy, is the Lord of host; The whole earth is full of His glory.
> And the posts of the door moved at the voice of him that cried, and the house was filled with smoke.
> Then said I, Woe is me! For I am undone; because I am a man of unclean lips, and I dwell in the midst of a people of unclean lips; for mine eyes have seen the King, the Lord of hosts.
> Then flew one of the seraphim unto me, having a live coal in his hand, which he had taken with the tongs off the altar;
> And he laid it upon my mouth, and said, lo, this hath touched thy lips; and thine iniquity is taken away, and thy sin purged.
> Also I heard the voice of the Lord, saying, Whom shall I send, and who will go for us? Then said I, (Isaiah) here am I; send me."
>
> Isaiah 6:1-8 (KJV)

Throwing off my blanket and jumping to my feet, I shouted: "That's it!" God had spoken to me through the prophet Isaiah. *Lord, I cried, I want to be an Isaiah! I, too, say as Isaiah said, here am I Lord, send me. I will go where You want me to go and I will do what You want me to do.*

When I first accepted Jesus as my Lord and Savior, the prophet Isaiah spoke loud and clear to me through chapter 30, verse 21: "Whether you turn to the right or to the left, your ears will hear a voice behind you, saying, "This is the way; walk in it." Now, Isaiah spoke to me again in chapter six. Incredible!

Immediately, I recalled the scripture my mother read to me as a child, Psalms 32:8 (KJV): "I will instruct thee and teach thee in the way which thou shalt go: I will guide thee with mine eye."

Excitement filled my being with the presence of the Lord. God spoke to me and my life would never be the same.

CHAPTER 3
CITY OF FAITH HOSPITAL
OR
PIT OF HELL

Nursing has proven to be a wonderful career. I have had the opportunity to work in many areas of the medical profession. Years working in MED-SURG (medical-surgical) laid the foundation for other specialties in my career. My curriculum vitae entail working as a 1st lieutenant in the U.S. Army, private-duty nursing with some home health care, infectious disease, school nursing, college nursing, hospice, and critical care nursing in the coronary care unit (CCU).

My desire to get serious about praying for my patients was at its peak when I began my critical care nursing. CCU nursing was always of interest to me. With a good background in nursing, I felt ready to make the leap into the big guns of the medical profession.

I applied for CCU nursing at two of our largest hospitals in my home town. Accepted at both, I made my decision and a start date was given. Excitement overflowed within me as I contemplated being a critical care nurse, a desire of my heart.

With my new nursing career in CCU starting in one month, some traveling was on the docket. My husband, Bill, had been planning a cross-country trip for the family for the past two years. It was summer vacation for the children, and Bill was graciously given four weeks off from work with no strings attached. Excitement filled the air as we threw our last suitcase in the back of our big, red, truck. Armed with my hefty train whistle, we were off and running. It was my job to blow the whistle every time we crossed a state border. Eventually, I was fired and replaced by our three children. They proved they were more than competent to be whistle blowers.

Each of the children chose a specific thing they wanted to do on our trip. Scott's dream was to see the San Francisco Giants play at Candlestick Park. Just days before, we gave Scott an official Giants jacket for his birthday; and he proudly wore it during the game. Ginger loved koala bears. Living on the East Coast never afforded her the opportunity to see them. We were off to the San Diego zoo, where another dream was fulfilled. Colette, our youngest at 10 ½ years, wanted to see the T V game show "Family Feud." Fulfilling this dream proved to be quite a challenge. Standing in line, waiting to go into the show, I quickly realized that children under the age of 15 were not permitted, even with their parents. I immediately started applying makeup to Colette's face and redoing her hairstyle. It worked. We all breathed a huge sigh of relief while taking our seats. Now, only one problem remained: my mouth. We were told that if we yelled out at any time during the show, we would be thrown out. To ensure this, we were given lollipops to suck on during the show. We all did great until my lollipop was gone. Without realizing it, and without a lollipop to suck on, I blurted out an answer. I didn't get caught and sat with my hands over my mouth for the remainder of the show. All of our children's dreams had come true. Our vacation was a success.

While driving through Oklahoma, we decided to stop at Oral Roberts University (ORU) so Scott could tour the college. In two years, Scott would be graduating from high school. We needed to get serious about selecting a Christian college. Our tour guide was very informative. During the tour, he pointed out the campus hospital, City of Faith. I couldn't believe it. A Christian hospital! How unique. Bill and I decided to tour the hospital immediately, while the children continued the tour of ORU. My heart leaped as we walked across the lawn to City of Faith Hospital. It was a brand-new, majestic, tall building that reflected the sun's rays as they danced off of thousands of windows of this architectural wonder. It was a masterpiece, with all the latest equipment. Ann was the student assigned to us for our tour. While touring the hospital, I decided to submit an application. I thought, who knows, maybe this is where God wants me. After all, I did pray that I would go where He wanted me to go and do what He wanted me to do. Asking Ann to excuse us for a few moments, I spoke with Bill about my idea of applying at this hospital.

Bill, tongue in cheek said, "Sure, if you want to commute 1,000 miles a day. Go for it."

So I did. I asked Ann to take us to the human resources department at the end of our tour. Ann was more than accommodating. After introducing us to Cindy, the head of the human resources department, Ann said her goodbyes. After I expressed a desire to work at City of Faith Hospital, Cindy was gracious enough to grant me an interview right on the spot. Bill waited patiently while I filled out the extensive application. I informed Cindy that I was interested in working in critical care. After reviewing my application, Cindy told me that every patient is admitted with a prayer partner. Cindy promised to let me know if I would be hired after my application was reviewed by their committee. Wow! I could pray with my patients. Surely, this must be what God wants for me.

Our family's travel adventures ended all too quickly. While back home unpacking and doing laundry, I was interrupted by the ringing of the phone.

It was Cindy from Human Resources at City of Faith Hospital. "We have reviewed your application and references and have decided to hire you. We would like you to start as soon as possible."

I was so excited, I could hardly speak. I couldn't believe they wanted to hire me. It was a whim that I even applied. *Lord, is this You?* My mind was flooded with questions. "Cindy, I have several issues I will need to take care of. I will call you back in a couple days with an answer."

Over the next few days, I was in constant prayer seeking the Lord's direction. I didn't hear the Lord say yes, and I didn't hear Him say no. However, there was one absolute. I did not have the peace of the Lord concerning this new position at the Christian hospital. My time was up. I had to call Cindy. Reluctantly, I dialed the number for City of Faith. Cindy answered the phone when I was transferred to Human Resources. I fought the tears upon hearing her voice.

"This is Cindy. May I help you?"

"Cindy, this is Georgia. I am sorry to tell you that the Lord has not given me the peace about working at City of Faith."

"Georgia, have you considered everything I told you on your interview? You can work in any department you would like. Remember, you will have complete freedom to pray with your patients."

"Cindy, I understand this. But if you need an answer now, my answer is no. I must have the peace of the Lord before I make a decision."

"Georgia, take a few more days. I understand. This is a big decision. We will wait to hear from you. We really would like you to be a part of our team. Talk with you soon. God Bless." CLICK!

Tears flowed down my cheeks. I wanted so much to go to the Christian hospital and pray for my patients. *God, why won't You give me an answer? I can't go if You don't release me. I can't step out without Your peace and assurance that this is Your will for my life. Please Lord, I want to go so much, I can taste it.*

Managing to regain my composure, I started to prepare dinner. So many thoughts swam through my head. *Dear Lord, in a few days, I am to start to work in my new position here at home. I was so excited when I was hired. Now, I just want to go to City of Faith. Will I be able to pray for patients at my new job? I know I can pray for them in the Christian hospital. I guess I should start to work here in CCU until I get the green light from You to go to City of Faith. What am I to do?*

The next three days quickly passed. God was silent. I had no choice but to call City of Faith with my sad news. Tomorrow, I would be starting to work in my hometown hospital. A decision had to be made now. The time had run out. Slowly, I dialed City of Faith. "Human Resources, please." I immediately recognized Cindy's voice when she answered the phone. "Cindy, this is Georgia. God has not given me His peace concerning working at your hospital. Therefore, until that happens, I am not able to come. I am committed to praying about coming and will let you know when I have a definite decision. I long to come but I must wait on the Lord for His will for my life. I promise to be in touch."

I will never forget this conversation with Cindy. It took all my strength just to dial the phone number. It was death to a vision-a vision of working in a Christian atmosphere where there would be total freedom to pray with my patients. God's silence was overwhelming to me. I was devastated and empty inside. Crying myself to sleep, with all hope gone, I surrendered the idea of ever praying with my patients.

Five A.M. came too soon. I was rudely awakened by my blaring alarm. My first day of orientation in CCU was here. A mixture of emotions overwhelmed me as I drove to the hospital. I was excited about my new adventure and also sad that I wasn't on my way to Oklahoma. The classes and instructor were great. It proved to be a very challenging six weeks of critical care classes, ending with a very difficult test. If I passed, I would be working in CCU. If I failed, I would not be given another chance to prove myself; never would I get to work in critical care. Every day after class I studied and studied and reviewed the material we had just received that day. This six-week course overwhelmed me. It consumed me. There was time for nothing else, and only a few hours of sleep every night. Finally, doomsday arrived. The six weeks of classes ended, and the test was the next day. Restless sleep with an anxious spirit left me weary in the morning. The drive to the hospital seemed to never end. Constantly, I rehearsed my notes, in my mind. Was I prepared? What else could I have done? My walk from the parking garage to the class room gave me time to breathe deeply, relax, and settle myself. Sitting with pencil in hand, I began answering the questions. The time passed quickly. We were alerted when only five minutes remained. Before I knew it, I was walking back to the parking garage.

It had been a day of incredible stress. Driving home, I finally began to relax. Surrendering my future to the Lord, I said, *Lord I will work wherever You want me to work. You know I would like to be in Oklahoma, but here is okay too. I would like to work in CCU, but if there is somewhere else You want to plant me, then that is also okay.*

Early the next morning, the phone was ringing off the hook. Grabbing the phone, I heard a voice say "Georgia, this is Mrs. Martin, your orientation instructor. I am pleased to tell you that you passed your exam and will be working in CCU. Report to CCU tomorrow at 7 A.M! Have a good day."

Again, I was both excited and sad. I was elated that I passed my exam and was qualified to work in CCU. However, this meant that I probably would not be going to City of Faith Hospital in Oklahoma. Yet, I still had hope that somehow, someway, sometime God would give me the green light and say, "GO!"

My first day in CCU was a little overwhelming. I arrived at 6:30 A.M. The nurse's report on each patient's condition would start promptly at 7:00 A.M. "Report was the time between shifts when a detailed account of every patient's condition was given to the staff coming on duty for the next shift. I sat quietly in a corner of the nurse's station waiting for the day shift to arrive. The number of machines and gadgets in each patient's room left little space for the nursing staff to maneuver while taking care of the patient. Noises coming from the ventilators, balloon pumps, and IVs, sounded like an orchestra tuning up for rehearsal. What a difference from your typical MED-SURG nursing unit. "Are you Georgia?"

"Yes I am."

"I am your nurse manager Ann. Report will be given in our conference room. Please make yourself comfortable, and I will be with you in just a minute."

Ann seemed so sweet and caring. Before report started, Ann introduced me to everyone. Report lasted 45 minutes. Details were the name of the game. Everything about each patient's condition was critical information and necessitated reporting. When report was finished, Ann introduced me to Ruthie.

"Ruthie will be your preceptor. She will orient you to Coronary Care. Ruthie will be with you for several months and on every shift you work. In other words, Ruthie will be your shadow. Georgia, there is a lot to learn, and you must be supervised until you master even the smallest detail."

Before I knew it, 3:30 P.M. arrived, which meant my first day in CCU was over. Driving home, I reflected on the events of the day. Ann seemed pleasant, but Ruthie, well, I was not so sure. At times, I sensed a tone of sarcasm in her voice when she spoke to me. I needed to put that behind me and give Ruthie a chance. It probably was just my imagination. All in all, it was a good first day.

Friday arrived before I knew it. My first week in CCU was over and I survived. I did it! Over the weekend, I found myself reflecting on my first week in CCU. A mixture of emotions filled my soul. It was great having the opportunity to work in critical care, something I always wanted to do. However, I had to admit that the atmosphere in CCU was a little disturbing. Much of this disturbance centered on report time. Report occurred between every shift change, three times a day. The charge nurse for the shift gave report on each patient's condition to the next shift of nurses. The seriousness of each patient's condition necessitated a lengthy reporting. Unfortunately, our small conference room was not ventilated. During our forty-five minute report, at each shift change, every nurse in our non-ventilated room smoked. All of the nurses frequently cursed, especially during report. A typical report usually included liberal use of the F-word to describe each patient's condition. Patients were not the only ones worthy of this description. The nurses who were not in the report room were also described with this title. As puffs of smoke and negative attitudes filled the air, breathing became a challenge for me after 45 minutes.

When report ended and the door to the conference room opened, stale, blue, smoke literally rolled out of the room, down the hall, and into the rooms of critical care patients. Of course, each nurse wore the aroma of smoke on her clothing as she entered the patient's room. Ironically, the doctors had been telling their patients that they had to stop smoking to stay alive and improve their health. These patients had just suffered a heart attack. If they wanted to live, smoking had to become a part of their past, and fast. Unfortunately, nurses who smelled like smoke combined with clouds of cigarette smoke drifting in their rooms did little to squelch their cravings. Being a good nurse, of course, I would reiterate and confirm what the doctor said about smoking.

This statement usually was followed by the recent heart attack victim screaming at me. "I can smell smoke on you! You have some nerve coming in here smelling like a smoke stack yourself and telling me not to smoke." This outburst always led to John Doe complaining of chest pain. His outrage then led to increasing the morphine drip. What a vicious cycle.

The private coronary care rooms encircled a central nurse's station. This layout made it easy to see into each patient's room while charting. You would think that an environment of peace and quiet would be what the doctor ordered for his patients; however, this CCU was a far cry from the norm. A radio blared hard rock music twenty-four hours a day where the unit clerk sat taking orders from the patients' charts. The music (if you can call it that) played loud enough that every patient could hear it whether they wanted to listen or not. I guess the best way to describe my coronary care unit would be to call it a "pit of hell." That, my friend, would be putting it mildly.

By the time I finished my eight-hour shift and arrived home, I was mentally and spiritually spent. All I could think about was the beautiful City of Faith Hospital in Tulsa, Oklahoma. When would God give me the green light to move? I was tired of smelling like smoke. I wearied of hard rock music. I was embarrassed when my patients pointed out the coronary hypocrisy of the medical personnel who smoked. Day after day, week after week, my pit of hell only seemed to grow worse. I would come home after my eight-hour shift, collapse in my living room chair, and cry.

Shortly thereafter, the phone would ring. "City of Faith calling," a cheerful voice always sang through the receiver. "This is Cindy from Human Resources. Is Georgia there?" the caller asked.

"Speaking," I responded.

"When are you going to decide about the position we have offered you?"

I always responded by telling City of Faith that I was indeed praying about a position with their hospital. I wanted to come and work for them, but God had not released me from my present position. I could not walk out in front of the Lord. I had to wait for His peace and guidance. There was a time in my past when I decided to do things my way. I refused to wait for the

Lord's direction, ventured out on my own, and fell flat on my face. I promised myself that I would never do that again, regardless of how tempting a situation might be. You have no idea how much I wanted to work in a Christian hospital, where I could pray with my patients. I absolutely hated where I was working, but God knew best. Until I heard loud and clear that I should go to Oklahoma, I would remain here. This scenario was repeated every day. Every day I responded to City of Faith with the same reply.

One day after work, I got a brain storm. What if I start to pack to show the Lord that I am serious about going to Oklahoma? Then, He will believe me and give me the peace, direction, and green light to go. Isn't it funny how we think we can manipulate God, the creator of this vast universe? I was on a mission, and nothing would stop me. Each day, I'd wake up, go to work in the pit of hell, drive home, cry, pack, talk to City of Faith, and pray. Finally, after weeks of calls and coaxing from City of Faith, they phoned once again. Cindy and I had become quite friendly over the past weeks. This time when I answered the phone, I noticed that Cindy's tone was much more persuasive and urgent.

"Georgia, I want you to come back to Tulsa for a more extensive interview. We believe you would be a good fit here at our hospital. You do realize that you have a choice as to whatever department you would like to work in? You will have complete freedom to pray with your patients. In fact, we encourage it. Of course, you remember that your children's college education will be paid for. I will put a plane ticket in the mail today for you. Where would you like to stay in Tulsa next Wednesday?"

Wow! Talk about a closing. I must say I was overwhelmed with Cindy's offer. I promised to get back to her as soon as possible.

Obviously, I needed to have a very serious talk with the Lord. After hanging up the phone, I stretched out prostrate on the floor of my kitchen.

Lord, I cried. What do You want me to do? I reminded the Lord that I had fasted and prayed and claimed the scripture in the book of the prophet Isaiah. I said, *Lord, I will go where You want me to go and do what You want me to do. When City of Faith Hospital invited me to be a part of their medical system, I believed this was of You. Why then have You not given me Your peace about this job? Remember, Lord, that I said that I want to pray with my patients and tell them of Your love. Where I am working now is horrible. I can hardly breathe there let alone offer a prayer for anyone. At City of Faith I could pray for my patients. What about the kids' college education? God—they said they would pay for all the children's college tuition. Cindy is rolling out the red carpet for me. Please, can I go to Oklahoma? They are begging me to come.*

Finally after my little temper tantrum, I got quiet before the Lord. I waited . . . and . . . waited . . . and waited.

Georgia . . ., I sensed the Lord said.

Yes Lord, I am listening.

You will not go to City of Faith Hospital in Tulsa, Oklahoma, because you will have your own City of Faith Hospital right where you are.

I jumped up off the floor and shouted, T*hank You, Lord! I don't know how You will turn a pit of hell into a City of Faith, but I do know that You can't lie. If You said You will do it, I know it will happen.*

I immediately called City of Faith Hospital.

"Cindy, this is Georgia. God just spoke to me. He said He will give me my own City of Faith right where I am. Honey, tear up my application. I am staying home."

For the first time in months, I finally felt the overflowing peace of the Lord. T*hank You, Jesus!*

Sometimes, going where the Lord wants us to go is actually staying right where we are. Again, I am reminded of what Isaiah said in chapter 55, verse 8: "For my thoughts are not your thoughts, neither are your ways my ways, declares the Lord."

CHAPTER 4
LOVE YOUR ENEMIES - REALLY?

M y hometown City of Faith! How did it all begin? Did it happen overnight? Did God just hand me a City of Faith Hospital on a silver platter? Did things improve immediately? Far from it! No! In fact, they got worse.

Ruthie, my preceptor, proved to be quite a challenge for me. She was twelve years younger and had not been endowed with the gift of patience (lucky me). Hatred is a powerful word; however, I can't think of another to describe how we felt about each other. Daily, the animosity between us seemed to increase.

One day, at the end of the 7 to 3 shift, I asked Ruthie if she would like to count narcotics. Narcotics are medications that are under the category of controlled substances. They relieve pain but can be highly addictive. Therefore, narcotics are kept locked in a secure cabinet. Every nursing unit is a little different in the arrangement of the narcotic record book. I must admit that I was a little nervous the first time I counted "narcs" in CCU. Ruthie opened the door to the narcotics cabinet while I opened the narcotics book. The narcotics book was actually a three-ring binder containing daily records of the unit's narcotic use. Basically, it was a very important document, and counting the narcotics was an important task, one not to be taken lightly. Even so, our book sat on a very narrow stretch of the medicine countertop. There was barely enough space to contain the book when it was open for use.

Ruthie yelled, "Percocet. Twenty!"

Demerol was listed on the first sheet of the narcotic book. It is an injectable medicine. I reasoned that, because Ruthie yelled "Percocet," which is an oral medicine, she must be starting the count with the oral narcs. I flipped the pages to the oral narcs in the back of the book just as Ruthie yelled, "Demerol. Twenty-five!"

Now, I was flipping the pages, back to the injectables, to find the Demerol, when I heard her grating voice say: "Darvocet. Ten!"

Here we go again, I thought. Flipping the pages back to the oral narcs, I bumped the three-ring narcotic binder that held the sheets together. The rings sprang apart, and the book hit the floor as narcotics pages flew everywhere. But Ruthie was still calling out the names of the narcs, apparently oblivious to me crawling around the floor as I gathered the pages. Just as I snapped the rings together with the narc book once again intact, Ruthie slammed the narcotic door shut, locking the cabinet. As she placed the keys in her vest pocket, Ruthie smiled, slapping my right cheek, and said, "Don't worry, one day you will be able to count narcotics."

The image of Jackie Gleason with his fist in the air, spouting, "One of these days, Alice!" filled my psyche. I really wanted to punch her out. I was so angry with her for making me look and feel stupid and inexperienced. I was angry with myself for not handling the situation better. Resentment and hate welled up inside me. Me, the born-again Christian who wants to pray with her patients! Me, the soldier of Christ who gave up a dream job in Oklahoma just to be harassed and once again experience hateful, sinful thoughts.

Ruthie and I were working the 11 to 7 shift. During my probation period, I was required to work all three shifts, 7 to 3, 3 to 11, and 11 to 7. Every nurse needs to know exactly what responsibilities are associated with each shift. The nurse manager always tried to assign the nurses to rotate only two shifts per schedule; however, at critical-times, we might be called to work a shift not usually on our schedule.

It was time for me to learn the charge duties. A priority in patient security in CCU was to always make sure that the monitor alarms in each patient's room were set correctly. The patient's monitor reveals how many times a patient's heart beats for every minute. The low alarm was set at 50 beats per minute; the high alarm was always set at 150 beats per minute. If a patient's heart rate dropped below 50, revealing brachycardia, the alarm would sound. If a patient's heart rate would rise above 150, revealing tachycardia or ventricular fibrillation, the alarm would also sound. Immediate action was required in these potentially dangerous situations. As a conscientious nurse learning charge duties, I always had an eye on the monitor alarms, eye-balling the low and high alarm to make sure they were exactly in place. It was tops on my priority list.

Before I knew it, 7 A.M. was rapidly approaching. Fine-tuning my report notes from the night shift, I noticed Ruthie talking with Ann, the nurse manager. I just knew that she was up to no good, but feeling confident about my performance as a charge nurse, I entered the report room. The nurses working the next shift had all taken their seats. Giving a thorough report of each patient's condition, I was satisfied with my first experience of being charge nurse in a CCU.

Upon opening the report room door, Ann, the nurse manager, motioned for me to come see her. "Georgia," she said, "Let's do rounds together so I can check off your performance." Entering room #1, my reflexes immediately caused me to eye-ball the patient's monitor alarms. I couldn't believe what I saw. The alarms were turned off. The low alarm was extended past zero to off. The high alarm was also extended past zero to off. The nurse manager was livid. "What is wrong in this room?" Ann shouted.

I was speechless and almost gasping for breath. I thought I was going to pass out. Shaking, perspiring, and as cold as a dead fish, I grabbed hold of the patient's bed rail for support. Finally, I regained my composure. Taking a deep breath I said, "I know the alarms were on in this patient's room every time I made my rounds."

Ann, dismissing my response, huffed past me as she turned to go into room #2. It was the exact same situation as in room #1. Pushing me aside, Ann made an immediate about-face and quickly marched into the remaining patients' rooms. Yep! You guessed it. Every alarm had been turned off in each patient's room while I was giving report. The nurse manager was furious. Of course, my words were meaningless regarding the alarm settings. The fact is, every alarm in the CCU had been turned off.

I remember being numb and totally paralyzed with fear and disbelief. My patients could have arrested and no alarms would have sounded while I was giving report. Incredible! My job, my career, and my future were at stake. The desire to be a critical care nurse was going down the drain, and fast. There was nothing I could do or say. It is what it is. The alarms were off, and I was responsible as the charge nurse. I stood there and took the tongue lashing from Ann, watching Ruthie grin as she glared and gloated at me from behind the nurse manager's shoulder.

The intensity of hatred I had for Ruthie was off the charts. It was so hard for me to believe that someone could dislike me to the point of jeopardizing every patient's life for a good forty-five minutes while I was giving report. I just didn't get it.

God promised me a City of Faith. How could this be possible? I must look like a student nurse to all the other nurses. From that day forward, I hated to go to work. I dreaded every day and questioned God and my ability to hear Him. Did I really hear the Lord say He would give me a City of Faith? Oh, how I longed to be at City of Faith Hospital in Tulsa.

I fell into a routine of doubt, despair, and dread. I cried myself to sleep each night, sometimes sobbing into the pillow and feeling very sorry for myself. I really tried not to hate or fear Ruthie. I wondered if I had heard God clearly. I wondered what my life would be like if I were working at City of Faith instead of this pit of hell. I felt like a Ping-Pong ball. One day I had been working the 7 to 3 shift, arriving home at about 5 P.M. I wasn't even home five minutes before that irritating phone call came, requesting me to report back to work at 11 P.M. "I haven't even been home long enough to greet my children and you want me to be back there in six hours."

"Georgia, due to decreased staff and increased patient acuity, you have to report back."

Even more difficult than working all night, with about three hours of sleep, was when I was scheduled for the night shift and had to stay over and work the day shift due to staff shortages. It felt like I lived my life in a tornado atmosphere with constant swinging shifts, no lunch breaks, bouncing through my rounds, and constantly deflecting the professional blows from Ruthie. I guess the most aggravating thing was when I finally arrived home after my shift, only to be called back because of the emergencies in CCU. I would jump in my car and race back to the hospital to find out that now I am not needed due to a decreased census. Usually the decrease in census was due to the death of patients. The environment in CCU was changing constantly. That's expected; however, it was an abuse to ask nurses to be on call twenty-four hours a day with no reimbursement for time spent and gasoline wasted driving back and forth to no avail in these situations. Welcome to critical care. It was exciting and exhausting.

My twenty-five minute daily commute to work found me praying fervently for guidance, help, protection, direction, and peace. Finally, I would stand in front of the closed double doors that led to the CCU and utter a final prayer: *Dear Lord, please go before me into CCU. Grant me favor with Ruthie, Ann, and my peers. Give me Your wisdom when dealing with Ruthie. I give this day to You. Help me, Lord. Amen.*

One day, after months of this routine of fear, tears, and prayers, something shifted and the Lord quietly spoke to my heart. He said He would turn the entire Ruthie fiasco upside down for His glory. God in His gentle way began to reveal that the situation would change when my attitude changed. To be honest, I didn't understand what God was trying to help me see. *My attitude! My attitude! What about Ruthie's?!* All I knew was that I wanted a City of Faith and I was stuck in a pit of hell.

At 10 A.M., we received word that a life-flight patient was being transported by helicopter from West Virginia to our hospital. It was routine for the life-flight helicopters to transport patients, in critical condition, from West Virginia to our hospital.

Ruthie grabbed my arm and yelled, "Let's go."

Off to the helicopter pad we ran to wait. Ruthie decided to make small talk. "Georgia, guess what?"

Unenthused, I reluctantly uttered, "What?"

"Tomorrow," Ruthie beamed, "is my first-year anniversary in the coronary care unit."

I bit my tongue to keep from saying something I would regret. I just couldn't share her excitement. I remained angry, bitter, annoyed, and fed-up with Ruthie's treatment of me. It was becoming too much for me to handle.

Our conversation was blessedly brief and ended with the landing of the helicopter. We quickly got the new patient up to CCU, and I forgot all about Ruthie's conversation. The rest of the shift sped by that day, and before I knew it, three-thirty had arrived.

Driving home, I entered my mental routine of reliving the day and second-guessing my every move: Did I sign out all of my narcotics? Were all the treatments documented? Were my nurse's notes in proper order? Did I forget anything that could be used against me? The angst, stress, and fear never seemed to end with the shift. Then suddenly I recalled Ruthie's conversation. In almost the same instant, I heard the Lord speak to me aloud. He practically shouted at me,

Georgia, buy Ruthie a cake!

Gunther, a baker in my neighborhood, was the best cake maker. He had become an expert in cake decorating. When I first visited his bake shop and requested bizarre decorations, Gunther was reluctant to attempt something out of the ordinary, always referring me to his custom mainstream photos. Encouraging him, I told Gunther he could do it. Before long, Gunther had a big sign hanging in the window of his shop, "Bring in your pictures, I can make any kind of cake." Overnight, he had a booming business.

Over the years, Gunther had made me cakes decorated with fantastic pictures, photographs, designs, poems, or even essays. Whatever design I walked in the door with, no matter how outlandish or original, Gunther was always eager and excited to put my vision onto icing. It never took too much thought to buy a Gunther cake. One day my nephew Benji affectionately called my old, red, truck with an eight foot bed, "The Glory Train." I thought that was fantastic and that we should celebrate it. "That's a great idea, Benji. Let's party!" Off to Gunther's Bake Shop we trucked. I ordered a cake with a train on it. Each car held the name and drawing of my three kids and each niece and nephew. In big letters, the cake read: "The Glory Train." All we needed now was the ice cream. It was a great party and not one crumb was left as evidence.

Georgia, buy Ruthie a cake.

There it was again, that same voice. Well, it didn't take me long to realize that had to be the devil talking. Why would the Lord want me to get a fabulous Gunther cake for the hateful Ruthie?

The voice or impression continued: *Buy Ruthie a cake.*

Swallowing, I said, *Lord, is that You?*

Yes, He said with a spark of glee in His voice.

I couldn't believe it. *Now wait just a minute,* I replied. *I want to get this perfectly clear. You want me to take my hard-earned money and buy Ruthie a cake?*

Yep, the gleeful impression said. I was so mad I could have spit. *Where have You been? Haven't You seen how she treats me? She constantly lies and tries to get me written up. And You want me to take my hard-earned money and buy her a cake? UNBELIEVABLE!*

Before I knew it, I was parked outside of Gunther's Bake Shop, still arguing with the Lord. *All right,* I said. *I'll buy the cake, but I won't have it decorated!* Grabbing my purse and slamming the car door, I found myself inside my favorite bakery. Gunther was all smiles as he greeted me with a big hug.

"Oh, Nurse Georgee, it is so nice to see you. What is the big occasion today?"

Muttering, I said, "It is my preceptor's first-year anniversary in the coronary care unit."

"Wonderful!" Gunther exclaimed. "What shall we have written on the cake?"

I wanted to yell "Nothing!" Standing there speechless for what seemed like hours, Gunther patiently waited, smiling the whole time, with his elbows resting on the counter top.

All of a sudden, the voice was there again. *Georgia, tell Ruthie that she is loved.*

My immediate response was, N*O! I don't love her! I'm not going to lie and say that I love her.*

But the Lord slowly said, *I . . . LOVE . . . HER. I . . . LOVE . . . HER.*

I remember just standing in Gunther's Bake Shop frozen in a moment of time. I was numb. Waves of shame flooded my being as I stood before the Lord, naked in His sight. *God, this is hard for me. I don't love Ruthie, but I realize that You love her. Let's go one step at a time.* I immediately recalled a Bible verse from Romans 5:8: "But God demonstrates His own love for us in this: While we were still sinners, Christ died for us."

I get it. Ruthie is a sinner, *and God loves her. I was a sinner saved by grace, and I don't love her.* I certainly am not proud of my feelings, but that is where I was. Therefore, the cake would reveal a truth that I wasn't able to verbalize. "Gunther, write on the cake*: Congratulations, Ruthie, You are loved.* Decorate it with the prettiest flowers you can make." I was able to manage and compromise my feelings by having the cake read that she was loved. Not by me, but by God. It really didn't matter to me whom Ruthie thought loved her. I just knew it wasn't me. However, buying the cake was a gigantic step of obedience for me. I wanted to be faithful to the Lord, but everyone has to draw the line somewhere. At that moment, I just couldn't say I loved Ruthie.

Gunther beamed while tilting the cake at an angle for me to read his work of art. The cake was absolutely stunning. When I took the money out of my wallet and put it in Gunther's hand, I was set free. It was like a spring sprung up from the bottom of my feet to the top of my head.

For the first night since I had started working with Ruthie, I didn't cry myself to sleep consumed with fear and stress. My mind was racing as I lay in my bed that night. *I can't believe what I did today. I, Nurse Georgee, bought Ruthie a cake. Am I losing my mind? And to boot, I told Gunther to write that she was loved. Lord, I pray that I heard You correctly. Believe me; that was the last thing I would possibly think of on my own. I'm sure I heard You say, "Buy Ruthie a cake." No matter, it's done. The cake is really from You. I am simply the messenger. I am really trying, Lord. I want to be obedient to You.*

Five-thirty A.M. was here before I knew it. I slept like a baby. Excitement filled my soul driving to work. I was so excited, that I forgot to pray my usual uptight prayer of trepidation. I couldn't have anyway. I felt so incredibly joyful! Arriving early so I could get the table prepared for the celebration; my heart was rapidly beating with anticipation. The night nurses were all busy going about their 6 A.M. duties. My presence was unnoticed due to the hubbub of last-minute labs and EKGs. When I finished, our conference room never looked better. Plates, plastic-ware, and napkins were all in place. Of course, the cake commanded the center of attention. The time had arrived for the report to be given. As the nurses walked into the conference room, they were all asking one another who brought the cake. I was silent. Everyone read the words on the cake. My eyes were on Ruthie. When she read the words on the cake telling her she was loved, she started to cry. Tears immediately filled my eyes.

Lord, I cried. *Can we start over?* It was at that moment that I realized what a wretched woman I had been. *I am so sorry, Lord. I can't believe all the evil thoughts I have been harboring toward Ruthie. And, why! Because she insulted me and made me feel like an idiot. Is that reason to hate someone? No! Of course not! Am I really saved? I love You so much, and look what I have been doing. No one else knows my thoughts, but You know them. Lord, I feel like such a hypocrite. My grief is overwhelming me. I am the Christian nurse, and I want to pray with my patients. No wonder You never gave me the freedom to pray with my patients. How could You possibly use me when I have been hiding hatred in my heart against one of Your created ones? I must become like You. You love everyone, even my Ruthies.*

Over the weeks, I had moaned to the Lord about my pit of hell. Temper tantrums had been my norm. *When was I going to be able to pray with my patients* was my mantra?

It's all about the cake and my attitude. It was Your way of revealing to me the pit of backsliding that had encompassed my life since I met Ruthie. Thank You, Lord, for being so patient with me! I tend to be a slow learner. I get it. I must learn to love unconditionally, just like You.

After dinner that night, I sat quietly before the Lord. Reflecting on the whole cake experience, I picked up my Bible and started to read the Sermon on the Mount in Matthew 5:38-39; 43-44 (KJV). The words of Jesus jumped off the pages of my Bible.

> "Ye have heard that it hath been said, An eye for an eye, and a tooth for a tooth: But I say unto you, That ye resist not evil: but whosoever shall smite thee on thy right cheek, turn to him the other also.
>
> Ye have heard that it hath been said, Thou shalt love thy neighbor, and hate thine enemy.
>
> But I say unto you, Love your enemies, bless them that curse you, do good to them that hate you, and pray for them which despitefully use you, and persecute you."

WOW! It was like this passage of scripture was written just for me. It said I should love my enemies. Now, let's see. Would Ruthie meet these qualifications? Hands down! Well, then. How am I to react to my Ruthies? The Bible said to love my Ruthies. I am called to bless my Ruthies. I am to be good to them, and pray for them. I got an "F" on this test. I failed miserably. I did everything wrong. The good news is that God forgives me and forgets all my wrong-doings. His love towards me never fails. He loves me forever, and I can't do anything to stop God from loving me. Tomorrow is the first day of the rest of my life, and I am actually looking forward to it.

Reflecting on my fourteen years of nursing in CCU, I now realize that Ruthie did have a good reason to be excited when she exclaimed to me that her first-year anniversary in CCU had arrived. Looking back at my pit of hell, I deduced that no one lasted a year in this environment. Six months was usually the norm.

Lord, forgive me for not being sensitive to Ruthie. Do with me as you wish. Teach me Lord to hear Your voice. Help me to love those that don't love me. Lord, I cried, I want to love my Ruthies. Where do I even begin?

I have come to realize that praying for our enemies is obviously the answer. My prayer focus had totally realigned itself. Now, instead of asking God to deliver me from my pit of hell, I found myself praying for it. Finally, I thought I was starting to understand this Christian walk.

God, You are so patient and good. Thank You for not giving up on me. It is good to start over again. Praise the Lord!

CHAPTER 5
MY FIRST PRAYER IN CCU

Amos was a patient in room 605. Ruthie and I were working the 7 to 3 shift. Doctor Stent was examining Amos. After reviewing the EKGs, blood chemistries, and echo report on Amos' chart, Doctor Stent yelled, "This patient needs an emergency cardiac catheterization. Have him sign the consent form and send him to the Cath lab immediately. I'm on my way to scrub up."

Ruthie scurried to the desk and fumbled through papers for the consent form. "Amos," Ruthie said. "You must sign this paper now so we can take you for a heart catheterization."

Amos, looking confused said, "I'm not letting anyone fool with my heart." Ruthie's begging and pleading was to no avail. The situation was escalating out of control. The more Ruthie begged the more defiant Amos became. It was during this tense situation that I sensed the Lord speaking to me.

Georgia, now is the time for you to say your first prayer in CCU.

WOW! What do you think my response was? Isn't this the moment I had been waiting for? For months, I had been asking the Lord to open the door for me to pray with my patients. At last, my answer to prayer had arrived. Wouldn't you assume that excitement would fill my being? I'm sorry and ashamed to admit that instead of excitement, fear gripped me. How could this be? *Lord, are You asking me to pray in front of Ruthie?*

God's gentle voice vibrated my being, saying, *Georgia, now is the time for you to say your first prayer in CCU.*

I found myself arguing with the Lord. *Why do I have to pray now, in front of Ruthie? Can't I be alone with a patient when I pray? Why does Ruthie have to be here?*

God's voice persisted, gently reminding me of the prayer I prayed at church camp: *Lord, here am I. Send me.*

Okay! You win. I will attempt to open my mouth and pray. Finally, I prayed silently. *Lord, help me. I am so scared. It's bad enough that Ruthie is standing on the other side of Amos' bed. Did You notice, Lord, that Amos' room, with the door wide open, is directly across from the nurse's station, where all the hubbub takes place?*

Reality was quickly before me. Sandy, the charge nurse, standing in the nurse's station, directly across from Amos' room, was screaming at the top of her lungs, "Ruthie, Dr. Stent is on the phone. He's in the Cath Lab wanting to know where in the world is his patient. What is going on in there? Do I have to come in there and take care of this myself?"

Perspiring, Ruthie was beside herself. I never saw her like this before. Ruthie, the mean, sarcastic preceptor, was visibly shaken and white as a ghost.

Amos was adamant. "No, no, I won't sign that paper. No one is going to mess with my heart, and that's that!"

Having received one more nudge from the Lord, I finally opened my mouth. "Amos," I whispered, "Could I say a prayer for you and ask God if you should have this test done?"

"Sure! Nurse Georgee."

"Let's hold hands," I said. I reached across the bed to take Ruthie's ice-cold shaking hand in mine. In very slow motion, finally the three of us were holding hands for everyone to see. *What was I thinking? Oh well, too late now.* I remember opening my mouth and uttering, "Dear Lord, help Amos. Amen." I prayed the shortest prayer I have ever prayed.

As soon as I said "Amen," Amos yelled, "Give me that pen so I can sign that paper. Let's get on with it." I couldn't believe it. It never entered my mind that Amos would reverse his decision because of a short prayer. I was simply trying to be obedient to the Lord. Ruthie looked as shocked as I was, and greatly relieved that Amos was now compliant with what his cardiologist ordered.

Saying my first prayer in CCU was extremely difficult. I always want to do things my way. The desire of my heart was to pray for my patients; however, I wanted it to be on my terms. It had never entered my mind that Ruthie would be present; let alone saying a prayer within the ears of the entire CCU staff. The Lord was putting me to the test to see if I really wanted to pray for my patients, even when circumstances were not ideal.

As Amos recuperated from his heart catheterization and recent heart attack, many opportunities were given me to share the love of God with Amos.

Ruthie and I were now working the 11 to 7 shift. It was 2 A.M. Patients were all resting quietly, except Amos. The monitor in the nurse's station revealed that Amos was fidgeting and apparently restless. The Lord nudged me to present Amos with the opportunity to surrender his life to Christ.

My charting, medications, and treatments were completed on all my patients. Receiving permission from Ruthie to spend some time with Amos, I slowly entered his room. I closed the door, pulled the curtain in front of the door, and breathed a sigh of relief. This was the first time I had been alone with a patient. It was great not having Ruthie breathing down my neck, looking for something to complain about. (Even after the cake, there still wasn't a great love between us.)

"Amos, over the past few days, I have shared with you the love of God. Would you like to have a relationship with Jesus?" I asked.

"Oh, Nurse Georgee, I'm ready, I'm ready."

I was so excited as I witnessed the enthusiasm of Amos. After I suggested that we hold hands while we pray, Amos eagerly reached for my hands. While instructing Amos to repeat the prayer after me, I noticed that the patient's call light on the wall had just come on. This didn't make sense to me. I was holding both of Amos' hands. *How could the call light come on?* Then it hit me. Ruthie and her cohorts at the nurses' station had put the light on. This way, they would be able to listen to my conversation with Amos. Fear enveloped me as I stood there holding Amos' hands while I stared at the call light, knowing that every word I said was being heard by all of the nurses on the unit. Images of Ruthie and the other nurses laughing, listening to me share the love of God with Amos, was overwhelming. My eyes were fixed on the call light, which now appeared larger than the sun. Speechless, motionless, and fearful, I was mesmerized with the continual vivid glowing of the call light. My imagination was running wild with visions of my peers laughing and mocking me as I prayed. I was totally paralyzed with fear.

Amos' words penetrated my ears as he relentlessly kept saying, "Nurse Georgee. . .Nurse Georgee, aren't you going to pray with me?"

Regaining composure and praying to God for strength, I finally opened my mouth. "Yes Amos, we will pray." Taking my eyes off the call light, I was able to focus on praying. "Amos, repeat this after me: Dear Lord Jesus, forgive me of my sins. Come into my heart. Thank You, Lord, for forgiving me and accepting me just the way I am. I love You, Jesus. Amen."

Amos responded immediately and repeated the entire prayer. Afterward, he smiled from ear to ear and radiated with the love of God. The joy of the Lord flooded his being.

Thank You, Lord, I prayed, *for all You have done.* Pulling the curtain open I realized that the living word of God did not stay in the tiny CCU room. The living word of God went out through the intercom to those who had ears to hear.

Reflecting on Amos' crying words, "Nurse Georgee, aren't you going to pray with me," I realized that the world is crying these same words. Is there anyone out there willing to pray with me? God is asking; CAN I GET A WITNESS?

Wanting to be a good witness for my precious Lord, I realized that first I had to earn the right to witness to a patient. I had to excel in my profession and be the best nurse I could be. I had to let the love of God shine through me and my work. Carrying the largest Bible I could find and announcing that I was a Christian and out to save the world wasn't the right way to be a witness for God. Actions speak louder than words. I had to work hard to keep the love of God towards others in my heart. I had to love the Ruthies and pray for them. I had to go the extra mile without being asked. WOW! Being a Christian in the work place is not easy. But then, God never promised that being a Christian anywhere in this world would be easy.

As the days, weeks, and months passed, things were slowly changing in CCU. Attitudes of nurses were changing. Some nurses were transferred off of the unit while new ones came. Swearing ceased. Nurses started to ask me to pray for their patients, even though I never made an announcement that I prayed. My patients apparently told other nurses that I prayed with them. Perhaps word spread through the intercom. When our patients were transferred out of CCU to a regular floor, they would ask for their prayers at night instead of their sleeping pills. It became normal for other units to call and request me to come and pray for a patient we had just transferred. God was doing a new thing in CCU. Nurses were surrendering their lives to Christ. Christian radio replaced the hard rock music. The peace of the Lord flowed throughout CCU. God's peace! Nothing can compare to it or replace it. When I surrendered my life to Jesus, the peace of God was the greatest gift I received.

After the episode with Amos and the intercom, things were refreshingly quiet. However, my desire to pray for my patients was still front and center. *Lord,* I prayed, *will You give me another opportunity to talk to my patients about You?*

CHAPTER 6
BE STILL AND LISTEN

C huck was up early and on his way to work. It seemed like any other day. However, at 1 P.M., Chuck's life changed dramatically. When Chuck grabbed his chest and fell to the floor, his Forman and other workers came to attention. They called 911, and CPR was initiated immediately. The medics arrived just as the Forman found a pulse on Chuck. With sirens blaring, and lights flashing, Chuck was transported quickly to my hospital. The medics were given instructions to get Chuck up to CCU as soon as possible. We were ready, with the ordered IV drips hung on their poles. Within minutes, Chuck was hooked up. He was awake, alert, and oriented. Dr. Miller, the cardiologist assigned to Chuck, was satisfied that Chuck was stable enough to proceed with an emergency cardiac catheterization. "Cath" results revealed that only one vessel, the right coronary artery (RCA), was blocked 75%. A stent was inserted without complications, and Chuck was sent back to CCU. Chuck, now pain-free, rested comfortably for the rest of the day.

I found myself asking the Lord if I could approach Chuck and pray for him. But where and how do I start? *Lord, do I ask him if he knows You? Do I ask him what church he goes to? Did his parents take him to church? Has anyone ever talked to him about God? Has he read the four spiritual laws?* The questions in my mind were like a nonstop recording. *What do I say, what do I do?*

Be still! Georgia, be still and listen. Get your eyes off of yourself and just listen to your patients. Give them a chance to talk, and listen to what they say.

The Lord was reprimanding me for being so self-centered. God revealed to me that by listening to my patients, I was actually permitting my patients to open up and share their life story, which can be a great introduction to the gospel message. God used Chuck to show me how to alleviate my fear just by listening so I could find an opening to start to witness.

On my next rounds, I found Chuck pain-free and comfortable. His vital signs were stable, with the monitor reading normal sinus rhythm with an occasional extra heartbeat, known as premature ventricular contraction (PVC). PVC's may be a single event, occur in pairs or may occur several times a minute. In these instances, there is no need for alarm. However, when three or more PVC's occur in a row, the patient is now presenting with an emergency situation called ventricular tachycardia (VT). Prolonged VT necessitates shocking a patient with direct-electrical current across the chest wall (cardioversion). Usually the VT is terminated when cardioversion is done.

O.K., Lord, here it goes. "Hi, Chuck. I'm Nurse Georgee. I will be taking care of you until 3 P.M. So, what happened to you? Tell me your story."

Chuck relayed his story about the chest pain at work, and then he said he passed out.

I then asked Chuck what kind of work he did.

Chuck said, "I'm a carpenter."

WOW! This one is really easy. "Chuck, do you know who the greatest carpenter in the world was?" Chuck was a little hesitant and wasn't sure how to answer the question. "Chuck, did you know that Jesus was a carpenter, just like his earthly father, Joseph? You remember Mary and Joseph?"

"Oh, sure. I remember that from Sunday school."

"Chuck, at Christmas, we celebrate the Christmas story about Mary, Joseph, and Jesus. Have you ever thought about the Christmas story and what it is all about?"

"No, I guess I never gave it much thought. We just get together as a family and give gifts. Sometimes we go see the big manger display downtown, you know, with the baby Jesus."

"Chuck, may I tell you the true meaning behind the Christmas story and why Jesus came to earth?" Chuck was all ears. While sharing the gospel message with Chuck, I mentioned how privileged he was to have the same occupation that Jesus had. Chuck expressed a desire to know Jesus as his Savior. He prayed and asked Jesus to come into his heart and to forgive him of his sins.

Chuck then said, "My life has changed. I am a new carpenter and will never see my work in the same old way again." *Thank You, Lord for teaching me to really listen to my patients!*

Enter Anna:

The next day, I was scheduled to work the 7 to 3 shift. It would be my first time as charge nurse, during the day, without supervision. This was the final test for my performance in CCU. If I passed, no longer would I need a preceptor peering over my shoulder. Good Bye Ruthie. Although elated that I was finally considered capable enough to manage the unit without supervision, I was terrified at the responsibility that lay at my feet. No second guessing. The buck stopped with me. All questions would come to me, and I would make all final decisions, with patient's lives hanging in the balance. I would be the one all doctors and nurses reported to. Over and over again, I rehearsed all I had learned during my preceptor training with Ruthie. Questions, questions, questions bombarded my mind. I tossed and turned all night.

Lord, I prayed. Help me to remember every important detail. I want to be the best nurse and bring glory to YOUR name. Help me respond appropriately to all emergencies and take charge when needed.

I thought the night would never end. At 4:30 A.M., I finally gave up. The alarm would be going off in a half-hour, so I might as well get my shower now and get on with it. The cold water running in the shower never got hot. Of all the days for the hot water heater to blow! I hoped that this was not a forewarning of things to come.

Just as I was about to burst into tears, I sensed God's presence. *Georgia, be still and know that I am Lord.* These words from Psalms 46:10 continually spoke to my spirit. "Be still and know that I am God." *Thank You, Lord. I needed a reminder.*

Driving to work, I found myself again reliving the night worries. Sometimes I do have trouble just trusting and putting my faith in God. My mind was racing with charge-duty details. Praying, I asked the Lord to once again saturate me with His holy presence.

Lord, this is the big one; charge nurse for the 7 to 3 shift. Dealing with all the cardiologists and surgeons, Lord, I need direction and wisdom.

Standing before the closed double doors to the CCU, I offered up the last rites. *It is now or never. I can't do this on my own. Lord, please go with me and help me to be the best nurse for You. AMEN!*

I made it through our 45 minute report, and it was time for me to make rounds on all the patients. Approaching Anna's room, I quickly reviewed my notes from report on her condition. Standing outside Anna's room, I heard her talking. No one was in the room with Anna. Who is she talking to? I could see that she was not on the phone. Anna continued to speak. Again, I scanned my report notes on Anna to see if anything was said about her being confused. There was nothing there.

While pondering this situation, I heard Anna say, "I wish I knew how to get there. I really want to go but I don't know how or where to begin."

I must admit I was a little miffed that Anna's confusion was not reported to me. Immediately, I sensed the Lord speaking to me. Georgia, be still and listen. LISTEN! So I did.

"I know that I am dying, but how do I get there? I really want to go."

Walking into her room I said, "Anna, are you talking about heaven?"

"YES!" Anna shouted. "Can you tell me about heaven? My doctor said I don't have long to live. I have tried to be a good person and go to church. I believe there is a heaven and would like to go there, but I don't know how."

"Anna, I would love to tell you how to get to heaven. Do you know that there is only one way to heaven?"

"Why no, I didn't know that."

"Anna, Jesus is the one and only way to heaven."

"Nurse Georgee, I believe in Jesus. Does that mean that I will go to heaven?"

"Anna, just believing in Jesus isn't enough. Everyone can believe that Jesus existed. History has proven this fact. The question is; do you know Jesus as your Lord and Savior? Have you ever invited Jesus into your heart and asked Him to forgive you of your sins?"

"Nobody ever told me this before. I went to church all my life, attending Sunday school and church faithfully. I read and heard about Jesus. I sang songs about Jesus. I repeated prayers about Jesus. But I never knew Him! Oh, Nurse Georgee, are you sure it's not too late for me to know Jesus? My doctor said I have only days to live. How could I have gone to church all my life and never realized it's all about Him? I feel so ashamed."

"Anna, Jesus loves you and wants to live His life through you. It is not too late. Do you remember the thief on the cross beside Jesus during the crucifixion?"

"Yes, yes I do remember that. Wow! If it wasn't too late for the thief, then it isn't too late for me. Is that what you are saying Nurse Georgee?"

"Anna that is exactly what I am saying. We can pray right now to Jesus, and you can have confidence that when you take your last breath here, you will be immediately in heaven with Jesus."

"Let's do it, Nurse Georgee."

"Anna, let's pray. I had Anna repeat the following prayer: "Dear Lord Jesus. Forgive me of my sins. Come into my heart. Thank You for wanting to live your life through me and forgiving me. I love You, Jesus. AMEN!"

"Nurse Georgee, will Jesus ever leave me? Do I need to say this pray every day?"

"Anna, Jesus promises to never leave us or forsake us. There is nothing you can do to have Jesus love you any less, and there is nothing you can do to have Jesus love you more. Do you remember the song from your Sunday school, Jesus loves me, this I know, for the Bible tells me so?" Anna immediately started singing this childhood song with a look of glory divine radiating from her small, emaciated face. "Anna, it's a done deal. You can have the assurance that now you know Jesus and you will be with Him forever. I need to finish my rounds. Perhaps after work we could continue this conversation. God Bless you, Anna."

Thank You, Lord, for teaching me to listen and not jump to my own conclusions! Thank You for Anna.

CHAPTER 7
TWO STEPS FORWARD, THREE STEPS BACK

R uthie and I were now working the 11 to 7 shift. My patient, Bill, was recovering nicely from his heart attack, and his condition was now stable. Transfer orders had been written for Bill to go to a regular unit in the hospital. He no longer would be confined to his bed, hooked up to a monitor, oxygen, or IV's. Excitement filled the air as Bill talked about his future and recuperation at home. Arrangements were being made for some cardiac rehabilitation at a facility close to Bill's house. Unfortunately, the hospital was filled to capacity and overflowing with patients in the emergency room who were waiting for beds. Bill was stuck in CCU.

After getting the report, I decided to do Bill's assessment first so he could settle in for the night. While walking to Bill's room, the Lord spoke to me. *Ask Bill if he knows Me.*

Okay, Lord. Let's give it a go. Bill's assessment was negative. Blood pressure was within normal limits. His heart was beating strong and regular at a rate of 78. Bill's enthusiasm was contagious as he talked about going home.

As Bill was telling me about his future plans, the Lord reminded me of the question I was to ask him: *Bill, do you know Jesus?*

Questions bombarded my mind. Do I just interrupt him and ask him God's question? Wouldn't I be putting a damper on his excitement about going home if I started talking about God? Removing the blood pressure cuff from his arm, I spotted a statue of the Virgin Mary on Bill's window sill. Oh no! Bill must be a Catholic. I am a Protestant. How can I share Jesus with Bill if he is of a different religion? Fear once again overwhelmed me. I didn't know what to say or where I should even begin. It was just like the call light on the wall in Amos' room. I thought I was over my fear of man. What is wrong with me? Am I ashamed of the gospel?

God interrupted my thoughts once again. *Ask Bill if he knows Me.*

Silently, I talked to the Lord and said, *I will ask Bill, but not tonight.* Frozen in fear as the statue of the Virgin Mary demanded my attention, I told the Lord, *There would be other opportunities to talk to Bill. Tonight I will be a great silent witness, excel in my nursing assessment, and wait for the right opportunity to talk with Bill.* I was off to my next patient.

Bill rang the call light two hours later.

Walking toward Bill's room, again, God spoke to me. *Georgia.* God's impression was so strong. It was like He was shouting at me. *Ask Bill if he knows Me.*

Okay, Lord. I do want to be obedient to You. Help me to say what You want me to say. "May I help you, Bill?"

"Nurse Georgee, I am tossing and turning. I guess I am so excited about going home soon."

Once again, I was preoccupied with the statue of the Virgin Mary. Bill's conversation was being drowned out by God's loud, relentless command, *Ask Bill if he knows Me.* Trying to ignore God's voice, I told Bill I would be back with a repeat sleeping pill. God's voice never let up. Confident in my silent witness approach, I told the Lord I would be the best nurse tonight. Fluffing the pillows just so, straightening the sheets with all wrinkles disappearing, fresh water in his bedside pitcher, and his call light securely fastened to the bedrail, Bill's room was perfect. Surely, my bedside nursing skills would cause Bill to ask me questions that would prompt a religious answer.

It was a relatively uneventful night. Bill's light came on for the third time. It was 5:30 A.M. Leaving the nurse's station to answer

Bill's call light, God spoke to me again. His voice was now stronger than ever. *Georgia, ask Bill if he knows Me!*

I immediately responded silently to God's request. *Lord, we have plenty of time. After all, Bill is stable and well enough to go home soon. I promise You that I will follow up with Bill a little at a time. Tomorrow, I will find out what unit they transferred him to. I will visit him and slowly get around to talking to him about You. I just can't come on too strongly. Lord, do You realize that I work with his wife in CCU? If I come on too strong and he tells his wife and she tells Ruthie, who tells my nurse manager, and she tells the supervisor, and I get written up, Lord, I could get fired. Why can't I just be a good silent witness tonight?* I was exhausted arguing with the Lord. Over and over and over again I heard the words, *Ask Bill if he knows Me.*

After addressing Bill's request, I took Bill's hands in mine and said, "Bill, if you need anything tonight, just ask Jesus." Whew! I actually said something about God. It was a step. Yes, maybe a baby step, but never the less a step. Actually, I felt pretty good about my witnessing performance. Surely, this would satisfy God. Tomorrow is another day. Tomorrow I will try and ask the question. I just need to do a little bit at a time.

Riding the elevator to the garage, I found myself smiling at how I witnessed to Bill. Maybe it wasn't what God wanted me to say, but at least I said something. I comforted myself with this thought. God was silent. It was a long ride home.

The phone was ringing as I entered my house. My nurse manager's voice sounded shaky as she tried to talk. "Georgia, a HALF-HOUR after you left the unit, Bill died. His wife is here, and she wants to see and talk to you."

"NO. . . NO. . . NO!" I yelled. "He couldn't have died. He was our most stable patient."

"Georgia, Bill died, and his wife needs you here right now."

I was in a state of shock. I couldn't believe it. How could this be? Regaining my composure, I said, "I'll be right there."

Racing to the hospital, I was reliving the night. I failed the test. God spoke to me loud and clear three times. I remember where I was standing each time I heard His voice. *Ask Bill if he knows Me.* FIVE WORDS! FIVE WORDS! I only had to say FIVE WORDS, "Bill, do you know Jesus?" and I couldn't do it. Three times, I refused to be obedient to the Lord. Driving was difficult due to the constant wiping away of the tears from my eyes. Yes, I can wipe away the tears, but I can't wipe away my disobedience. Oh God, can You ever forgive me for not listening to You? I am so sorry.

Jesus, for the first time in my life, I realize how Peter must have felt when he denied You three-times. Peter told You how much he loved You. I also tell You every day how much I love You. Yet, when Peter was faced with arrest, he said, "I don't even know Him." When I was faced with the fear of losing my job, I said nothing. I refused to be a witness for You, my God and Savior, Jesus Christ. God, You gave me three opportunities to be a witness for You. All I had to do was open my mouth and say five words. Bill, do you know Jesus? I let the fear of man override my obedience to You Lord. I just couldn't say it. I am so ashamed.

I don't remember ever crying as deeply as I did that day driving back to the hospital. It felt at times as though I was gasping for breath. At one point, I had to pull off to the side of the road because I couldn't see through the tears. The remorse I felt was almost unbearable. Bowing my head in prayer, I asked Jesus to forgive me, not that I deserved to be forgiven. I didn't. Because of His mercy and grace, He is always ready to forgive us before we even ask. What a wonderful Savior.

So many times I ponder why Jesus wants to have anything to do with me. Often I recall my time at Jumonville when I told the Lord that I wanted to be an Isaiah and go where He wanted me to go and do what He wanted me to do. Words are cheap, and most of the time just empty. However, God in His mercy gave me a wonderful opportunity to be a witness for Him. How did I respond? I didn't. I blew it big time. Not only did I blow an opportunity to be a witness for God, I had the audacity to tell God that we had plenty of time; that I knew best what to say and when to say it. God knew Bill's time here on earth was limited. I didn't need to have this information. I needed to obey God.

Somehow, I managed to get myself together despite the red face and puffy eyes. Bill's wife Patty was waiting for me in our little kitchen in CCU. Patty ran to greet me, falling in my arms. We just stood there in each other's embrace, crying. Finally Patty reached for a chair and collapsed like a wet noodle. She did most of the talking, and I listened for a change. Sipping her coffee, she enjoyed reminiscing about Bill's life. A very interesting thing happened during our conversation. Patty reached into her large bag of Bill's belongings and pulled out the statue of the Virgin Mary. "Georgia, I am Catholic and thought that maybe this statue would help comfort Bill while he was here, even though he was a protestant."

How do you like that? My fears were totally lies from the enemy. Bill's religion was the same as mine. If I would have been obedient to the Lord and did what God wanted me to, I could have become aware of this knowledge.

I shared the love of Jesus with Patty and gave her a pamphlet about salvation to take home. We prayed and slowly walked to the garage. Waving goodbye as we parted ways, I started crying uncontrollably. I just couldn't believe how I disobeyed the Lord. While sitting in my parked car in the garage I prayed, pleaded, and begged the Lord to forgive me. I didn't hear His voice. But, I just knew that I was forgiven. I promised the Lord if He would just give me another opportunity to tell someone about Him, I would never again refuse to do so. The desire of my heart was to be a good witness for Jesus. I longed to tell my patients about Jesus. *Help me; Lord, in this process. Teach me Thy ways. Show me the path You want me to take. Fill my mouth and guide my steps. I want to be righteous in Thy site.*

What did I learn from this experience? The Lord showed me that when I talk to someone about Him, I am not talking about a religion. I am introducing them to my Lord. We don't even need to discuss religion. Caught up in what I thought were differences in our religions, I missed a wonderful opportunity to introduce Bill to Jesus. Yet, we have a God that willingly gives us a second chance. He never gives up on us, and He never will. God is so good!

CHAPTER 8
ENTER JOE – ANOTHER CHANCE

Pastor Dave, a Methodist minister, called and asked me to visit one of his parishioners. "Georgia, Joe is in the Burn Unit of your hospital. I have tried many times to visit him to no avail. Every time I go to the hospital, the nurses tell me it's not a good time for a visit. It seems they are always changing his bandages and doing treatments. The nurses can't even give me an appointment time to see Joe. Georgia, Joe is in critical condition. He has been so faithful in his church attendance. However, Georgia, Joe never surrendered his life to Jesus. My prayer is that he would be given one last opportunity to receive Jesus as his Savior. I never pushed Joe on the subject of his salvation. Joe was young and in good health. It seemed that we had plenty of time for this decision. Now he is at death's door without a Savior. Georgia, I feel so guilty that I wasn't more persistent in my sermons about a relationship one can have with Jesus. I am asking you to please see if the Burn Unit nurses will let you see Joe. I don't know what else to do."

"Pastor Dave, of course I will see Joe. In fact, today I am working a double-shift starting at 3 P.M. I will be there for sixteen hours. Surely, I will see Joe during that time." "Oh Georgia, that's wonderful. Tell Joe that I sent you and that the whole church is praying for him. Thank you so much. You are in my prayers."

"Pastor Dave, just yesterday I prayed and asked God if He would give me another chance to pray for a patient. God has used you to answer my prayer. I, too, am feeling guilty. Less than twenty-four hours ago, I failed to witness to a patient about the love of Jesus. Jesus asked me three different times to ask my patient if he knew Jesus. Three times! Pastor Dave, I was silent. I never asked the question before my patient died. The remorse is overwhelming. Thank you for your call. I will keep in touch. God bless."

Arriving at the hospital thirty minutes before I started my shift, I was thrilled at the opportunity God had given me. *You did forgive me. You have given me a second chance. Thank You, Lord. You are so good.* I made a bee line to the Burn Unit.

After introducing myself to the charge nurse, I asked permission to see Joe, explaining the situation that took place with his pastor. Cheryl remembered meeting Pastor Dave and apologized for all the inconvenience he experienced. "Let me see if you can visit with Joe now." Cheryl called Joe's room, checking with his nurse about my visit. The answer was no. "I'm sorry Georgia. Joe requires constant care. Perhaps you can come later."

"That's fine. I will be here for the next sixteen hours. I work in CCU. Please have his nurse call me as soon as I can see him. Thanks."

It was a busy 3 to 11 shift, with several acute admissions. While giving report at 11 P.M., I realized that the Burn Unit hadn't called. Now, I was getting anxious. I quietly offered a prayer for Joe and prayed they wouldn't forget about me. The busyness in CCU continued throughout the night. This was good. It kept my mind occupied on my work and not Joe; until 2 A.M., at which time I gave in and called the Burn Unit, asking to speak to Joe's nurse. Cathy, Joe's nurse, was very pleasant. "No, Georgia, we haven't forgotten about you. We are incredibly busy. I promise I will call you tonight." Before I knew it, 5 A.M. arrived with no call. I did not take a break during the night so that I could use that time to visit Joe.

At 5:30 A.M., the phone at the nurse's station was ringing off the hook. It was Cathy at the Burn Unit. Hallelujah! "Georgia, you can visit Joe right now." "I'm coming." I notified the staff that I was taking my break now and ran to the Burn Unit. Excitement filled the air. *God, You are giving me a second chance to prove to*

You how much I love You. I want to be obedient to Your call and be the witness You have called me to be. Thank You for another chance. Help me, Lord, when I talk to Joe.

Cathy escorted me to Joe's room. It was a semi-private room. There was another patient in Joe's room. It never entered my mind that another patient would be in Joe's room. In CCU, our rooms are private. Now, I have to talk to Joe with another patient in the room. I was starting to feel a little uneasy when reality struck. Following Cathy to Joe's bed by the window, I was shocked at what I saw. There were seven nurses around Joe's bed, removing bandages, applying cream to burned areas, and securing and re-taping his endotracheal tube. I thought I would pass out. How could this be, so-o-o- many people in Joe's room? Not only would I have to settle for another patient in Joe's room, but seven nurses. Give me a break. I made an immediate about-face and started to run out of Joe's room, saying "I'll come back later."

Cathy literally reached out and grabbed my arm as I was flying past her. "Georgia, if you leave now you will not have another opportunity tonight to see Joe. We are so busy. Don't you get it? We granted you this opportunity because of Joe's pastor. Are you going to pray for Joe? If you are, you better pray right now. I will not call you again." Cathy sounded so mean. I was literally frozen from fear at the sight of all these people. They apparently were not going to leave Joe's room when I prayed, which meant that I would be praying in front of another patient and Joe's seven nurses. Lord, have mercy! "Well!" Cathy exclaimed, "Are you going to leave or pray?"

It was at this moment that the Lord quietly reminded me of my request for a second chance. *Yeah! But Lord, in front of all these people?*

Now would be a good time for a fire drill. God was not amused.

His steady, strong voice continued to speak to me. *Georgia, this is your second chance. Do things always have to be your way? Do you want to be My witness? Then, pray.*

Okay, Lord. Here it goes. I am scared to death. However, I know that You will help me and fill my mouth. Slowly, I walked to the foot of Joe's bed. Waving my hand, I said "Hi, Joe." Joe was completely alert. He nodded his head to acknowledge me. Joe couldn't speak because he was on a ventilator, with a tube down his throat to help him breathe. "Joe, your pastor asked me to pray with you. Is that okay?" Joe nodded his head. "Joe, do you know Jesus?" This time Joe nodded his head no. "Would you like to know Jesus?" Joe nodded his head yes. It was at that point that I walked to the head of the bed. Joe was bandaged from the top of his head to the bottom of his feet. Only his eye sockets, mouth, and right ear were exposed. Cupping my hands around his right ear I whispered, "Joe, repeat this after me. Dear Lord Jesus." I felt a tapping on my left shoulder. It was the nurse at the head of Joe's bed. I glanced up not knowing why she was tapping my shoulder.

"Georgia, you need to speak louder when you talk to Joe. He can't hear you when you whisper."

Fine! I again cupped my hands around Joe's right ear and spoke a little louder; however I was still speaking in a whisper. I was so scared. I tried to speak louder, but I just couldn't. I guess I spoke in a louder voice at the foot of the bed when I was first addressing Joe. I wasn't praying then. I admit that I was ashamed of praying to God in front of all these nurses.

"Joe, repeat this after me." There it was again, the tapping on my shoulder. Now, what could be the problem? I glanced up at the nurse at the head of Joe's bed and said, "Yes?"

"Georgia," she barked, "Obviously, you didn't understand what I told you. Joe's hearing was damaged in the steel accident. When we speak to Joe, we don't whisper. So, why don't you just yell and get on with it."

Wonderful! *God, I know You are in control and I did ask You for another chance. This isn't exactly what I wanted, but then again, it isn't about me. If I lose my job, I am sure You will get me another one. If they admit me to the Psyche Unit, I'm sure You will take care of it. Okay, Lord, here it goes.* For the third time, I bent over, cupped my hands around Joe's right ear, and yelled, at the top of my lungs, "Joe, repeat this after me: Dear Lord Jesus." I paused to look at Joe's lips. They were moving. Hallelujah! Joe was repeating the words. He heard me. Who am I kidding? Everyone in the Burn Unit heard me. Not my problem. I continued to yell in Joe's ear.

"Forgive me of my sins. Thank You, Jesus, for forgiving me. Come into my heart. I give myself to You. I love You, Jesus. Amen."

Taking a deep breath, I stood up and noticed that every nurse around Joe's bed looked like a statue. I saluted the nurses, made an about-face, and walked out of Joe's room. My break time just ended. It was perfect timing. My body was shaking almost uncontrollably as I walked back to CCU. Breathing a sigh of relief, I offered a silent prayer to the Lord. *Thank You, Lord, for helping me to pray with Joe. I was so scared. Thank You for giving me the strength to be Your witness even when the situation is not ideal.*

I was excited that I was able to follow through and pray for Joe. I was given another chance. As I wrapped up my night duties, I was called to the phone in the nurse's station.

"Georgia, this is Cathy from the Burn Unit. You were just here and prayed for Joe. Georgia, a HALF-HOUR after you left, Joe died." I couldn't believe it. It was the exact same situation that happened with Bill in CCU. One half-hour after I left CCU, Bill died. God did give me another opportunity to prove my obedience to Him. The circumstances were the same. I blew the first opportunity to witness to my patient Bill. I almost blew my second chance to be a witness for the Lord with Joe. Thanks be to God for His strength and encouragement. This school of obedience that I am being trained in is not easy. But then, God never said it would be.

As I reflect on my witnessing experiences, I must admit that I never realized how self-absorbed I have been. The desire of my heart was to be a witness for Jesus. I prayed for years for the Lord to teach me and help me pray with my patients. Now, I find myself questioning if this really has been a true desire of my heart. What was my motive? It seems that every time God gave me an opportunity to pray, I found myself arguing with God, always questioning God about the circumstances. Was He sure that this was the time to offer a prayer? Why would God put up with me? I was always second guessing Him. My answer to His prompting me to pray was, "Now, are you sure?" *God, why do You even bother with me? I am such a miserable witness for You. Please don't give up on me. I love You, Jesus, and I want to serve You with all my heart. Teach me to die to myself and live for You. I want to be obedient. Help me to fear You more than man.*

God put up with me because of His unconditional love for me. He never gave up on me. Thank You, Lord, for your steadfastness. You are awesome.

When God asked me to ask Bill if he knew Jesus, no one else was around. Ruthie wasn't even in the room—just me and Bill! I couldn't open my mouth because of a statue and the fear of being reported. I failed. Yet, God in His mercy gave me another chance with Joe. I almost blew this one, too. Praying to God for another chance to be His witness became routine. God is patient. Hour by hour, day by day, God slowly guided me in my prayer journey with patients. As doors opened, I realized that I was not alone when it came to witnessing to my patients. He is always with me. He promised to never leave me. Before, I was relying on myself, witnessing on my own strength. It's different now. When an opportunity arises for me to offer a prayer to a patient, I now know that it is only through the power of the Holy Spirit that a prayer can be offered. It is not by my might or power that witnessing will take place. If God ordains it, witnessing will happen. It has nothing to do with me. This knowledge has been so freeing.

If we are willing to be His witness, God is able to do marvelous things in our lives. We serve a wonderful Savior. His mercy and patience is never-ending. Don't beat yourself up for your failures in witnessing. In God's eyes, there are no failures. If God can forgive me and use me as His witness, He can use anyone. He is looking for yielded vessels. WILL YOU BE A WITNESS FOR THE KING OF KINGS AND LORD OF LORDS?

CAN I GET A WITNESS?

CHAPTER 9
BIG JOHN - I SAW JESUS

Yelling at the top of his lungs, John screamed, "Nurse Georgee, get in here!" All the nursing staff raced with me to John's room. We all had been involved in his CPR and knew it was a miracle that John was still alive. What solicited John's screaming? Was he again experiencing chest pain? "John . . . John . . . what's wrong?"

John was a 40 year old man, flown by helicopter to us from West Virginia. His condition was extremely unstable, necessitating transfer to a big city hospital. The life-flight crew remained in charge, barking orders at Ruthie and me as they leaped from the helicopter. "Lead the way. We have to stay with John until he is in CCU. His heart stopped five times during flight. Run as fast as you can."

Ruthie and I were yelling, "Emergency! Move it! Out of the way!" to everyone in our path, as we raced like marathon runners to the CCU finish line. Ruthie and I literally threw ourselves against the two, large, mahogany doors that led to the entrance to CCU. The noise from the doors hitting the walls as they opened was deafening. All CCU staff immediately came to attention as we raced into John's new home. Within minutes, John was hooked up to the CCU monitor, had a Swan-Ganz catheter inserted with new IVs hanging, and new CPR patches applied to his chest. John presented as a perfect text book picture. We were ready and able for anything that might happen, or so we thought.

The life-flight crew was now gone. John was resting as comfortable as possible with his blood pressure stabilized at 118/80. His heart rate, at 88, continued to have some extra beats (PVC's), with intermittent short runs of ventricular tachycardia (VT). The atmosphere in his room was now one of serenity. Formally introducing myself, I oriented John to his new home. While bathing John, I sensed that the Lord was asking me to talk to John about his relationship with God. *Okay, Lord, I will do it. You gave me another chance with Joe. Thank You for this opportunity.* "John, has anyone ever introduced you to Jesus?"

Scratching his head with a somewhat puzzled look on his face, John slowly responded, "No, I don't reckon anybody ever has."

"John, may I introduce you to Jesus?"

"Sure."

Sharing with John for only a minute or two what Jesus did in my life, John interrupted me.

"Now wait just a minute, Nurse Georgee. I just don't know about this Jesus. I have never been in church. In fact, I have never even seen a Bible. I just don't know about Jesus."

"John, that's okay."

"Nurse Georgee, you don't know what I have done. Don't get me wrong. I have been laying here thinking about my life. I want to change. I don't want to beat my wife up anymore. I have been in terrible fights with the guys. I need to think about some things. I just don't know about this Jesus."

"John, that's fine. If and when you are ready to talk about Jesus, you know where I am."

John fell asleep for about an hour. Alarms started blaring, and the monitor showed that John was in VT, with a heart rate of 196, which increased rapidly into ventricular fibrillation. All CCU staff responded immediately with the typical CPR. Chest compressions, proper ventilation, and shocking John's heart all seemed to be to no avail. We were losing him, and fast. Even the IV pressors didn't help raise his blood pressure, which was nearly nonexistent. According to his monitor, John was flat-lining. No heart rate, no blood pressure, and no response to the repeated shocking at even 400 joules of electricity. We refused to give up. I don't remember how long we worked on John. It seemed like an eternity. The flat-line was engrained in John's monitor and was not disappearing. No rhythm was in site. Just as we were about to call it quits, John's monitor revealed a rhythm. John was coming back, unconscious, but back and breathing on his own.

Report time was rapidly approaching. Gathering my nurse's notes, my mind was racing with John's last words to me. "I just don't know about this Jesus." Report went well; however, it was longer than usual. I had a few loose ends to tie up before leaving for home. After getting my purse, I gave John's monitor one last glance. All seemed well. Breathing a sigh of relief, I was off. Placing my hand on the big doors to CCU, I was stopped dead in my tracks. John's loud demanding voice echoed throughout CCU.

"NURSE GEORGEE...E...E...NURSE GEORGEE...E...E, get in here." Immediately, I turned and ran to John's room. I heard my name bouncing off the walls surrounding CCU.

"John, I'm here. What's wrong?"

"I SAW JESUS! I SAW JESUS!"

"Oh John! What did He look like? I never saw Him. What color were His eyes, His hair?"

"I can't tell you that. All I know is that He is love. Look, He's here," pointing to the left side of his bed. "You want to know something? That devil is a mean devil."

"What do you mean John?"

"You know all those fights I told you I was in? Well, I never fought so hard as I did with that devil. I was sweating buckets full. That devil almost got me, but Jesus saved me. So, then I asked Jesus if I could come back for a little bit. So then, Jesus went through the gate to the Dad and asked the Dad if I could come back."

It was at this point that I felt it necessary to interrupt John and inform him that Jesus went to the Father. I thought it necessary to have a theological discussion about the trinity.

"Nurse Georgee, Jesus went to the DAD. He went to the DAD."

I heard the Lord yell at me as loudly as John screamed my name earlier, *GEORGIA, BE QUIET. LISTEN TO JOHN.*

But I just had to ask one more question. "John, did you see the Dad?"

"Oh no, I didn't see the Dad, but I heard the Dad."

"What did the Dad sound like?"

"Well. . . I guess it was like He was talking through a great big megaphone."

"WOW! You mean like thunder?"

"Yeah, that's what the Dad sounded like." Then, John sat straight up in bed and pointed his finger at me, commanding my attention. "Nurse Georgee, I want you to know something. No one goes through that gate to the Dad unless Jesus takes them."

I literally froze in amazement at what John just said to me. I'm sure my eyes were as big as cantaloupes. John had quoted my favorite scripture in the Bible. It is found in the book of the gospel of John chapter 14, verse 6:

> Jesus answered, "I am the way and the truth and the life. No one comes to the Father except through me."

My mind was racing with questions. John told me before his cardiac arrest that he never saw a Bible. He said he was never in church. Yet, he was quoting from the Bible a truth that I knew. How could this be? He couldn't be making it up. He knew nothing about the Bible. Did he really see Jesus? I was so confused. I am ashamed to admit that I doubted his account of what happened to him. Was John hallucinating? When he said Jesus went to the Dad, I asked John if he saw the Dad. I asked him that question because I doubted his story. The Bible tells us in the gospel of John chapter 6, verse 46:

> "No one has seen the Father except the one (Jesus) who is from God; only He has seen the Father."

I knew this passage of scripture. Therefore, if John would have said he saw the Father, then I would know he was hallucinating. *God forgive me. Why do You even bother with me? I battle fears, doubts, and unbelief. Is there any hope for me? Forgive me for doubting You.*

John continued to yell at me at the top of his lungs. "Nurse Georgee, I'm telling you the truth. NO ONE GOES THROUGH THE GATE TO THE DAD UNLESS JESUS TAKES THEM!" It was like John knew I doubted his story. How much clearer can it be? JOHN SAW

JESUS. Glory be to God. John had an encounter with the King of kings and the Lord of lords. Who am I to discredit his encounter? God forgive me.

Again, John very emphatically yelled, "Nurse Georgee, I'm telling you the truth. NO ONE GOES THROUGH THE GATE TO THE DAD UNLESS JESUS TAKES THEM. You don't believe me. Nurse Georgee, I'm telling you the truth."

"John, I believe. I believe." Once John knew that I finally believed him, he was ready to tell the world he saw Jesus and that Jesus was for real. With the door wide open to John's room and the nurse's station within ear shot, John yelled as loud as he could, "Is there anyone out there that doesn't know Jesus?" Immediately, all staff and even some visitors gathered in John's room. John radiated while he related his encounter with Jesus. Even his dear wife, who sat quietly in the corner of John's room, took it all in.

Eventually, John's room was cleared of nurses and visitors; however, the presence of Christ continued to permeate the atmosphere.

"John, let's talk about what just happened to you. Jesus revealed Himself to you as the Lord of lords and the King of kings. John, are you now ready to surrender your life to Jesus?"

"I sure am. What do I need to do? I know that Jesus is for real. I want to be with Him forever."

"John, you need to pray and invite Jesus into your life. You don't need to worry about fancy words. Talk to Jesus just like you talk to me."

"O.K. Nurse Georgee, here it goes. Jesus, it's John, the one you just saved from the devil. Don't leave me Jesus. Forgive me of all the fights I was in. Sorry I beat my wife up. Come live in me. Thank You for loving me. I'm YOURS. Amen!"

God, You are so amazing and awesome. Thank You for giving me the privilege to talk with a patient who has been in your presence. You have blessed me beyond belief. I know without a doubt that every word is true in the Bible. Sorry it has taken me so long. Thank You again for Your patience with me.

CHAPTER 10
MEET OUR 94-YEAR-OLD JEWISH LADY

S ophie, a 94-year-old Jewish lady, was admitted to CCU with complete heart blockage. This critical situation demanded immediate intervention. The electrical system in Sophie's heart was damaged. Therefore, her heart could not pump normally to sustain life. Only the insertion of a pacemaker could save Sophie's life. Since Sophie was hanging onto life by a thread, sending her to the operating room was out of the question. She would have died on the table. Time was of the essence. Sophie needed a temporary pacemaker inserted immediately until she would be stable enough to go to the operating room for a permanent pacemaker.

Dr. Adams, chief cardiologist, was immediately paged. I prepared Sophie for insertion of a temporary pacemaker. Within minutes of Sophie's arrival in CCU, Dr. Adams was cleansing Sophie's skin with betadine solution. The monitor revealed a heart rate of 35. Normal rate is 72–80. Remarkably, Sophie remained awake, alert, and oriented. Dr. Adams tried inserting the pacemaker wire several times to no avail. Sophie remained awake, but her heart rate was dropping. While Sophie's heart rate dropped to 34 – 33 – 32, she let out a horrible scream. Dr. Adams shook Sophie and yelled, "Sophie . . . Sophie, are you O.K?"

Slowly responding, she said "Y. . .E . . .S."

"Am I hurting you?"

"N . . .O."

Perspiration was dripping from Dr. Adams' forehead. Again, he attempted to insert the temporary pacemaker wire. Her heart rate was now at 31. LOUD EERIE SCREAMS again flowed out of Sophie's mouth. We were losing Sophie fast.

Dr. Adams began shaking her while yelling, "Sophie . . . Sophie, are you O.K.?"

Again, Sophie very lethargically responded in a whisper, "Y . . .E . . .S."

"Am I hurting you?"

"N . . .O."

Dr. Adams looked across the bed at me, shrugging his shoulders with a look of bewilderment. I was just as confused. Her heart rate was now at 29 and falling quickly. Why was Sophie letting out these loud eerie screams if Dr. Adams was not hurting her? It was at that moment that the Lord spoke to me and said, *Georgia, Sophie is being pulled into Hell.* Again, Sophie let out that heart-wrenching, horrible scream for the third time.

I immediately prayed silently and asked the Lord to spare her life. I said, *Lord, I promise You that I will tell Sophie that You are the true MESSIAH and that You love her.* Instantly at the end of my silent prayer, Dr. Adams had the temporary pacemaker wire in place. Connecting the wire to the pulse generator, I set the rate at 72. Our eyes glued to the monitor. We saw that the insertion had been successful. Sophie's heart rate was now at 72. Sophie's life was spared. Dr. Adams looked like a wet noodle. Talk about stressful situations. Welcome to CCU.

The next day Sophie was resting quietly, in stable condition. Dr. Adams decided to send Sophie for her permanent pacemaker. After signing the consent for surgery, Sophie was sent to the OR. Despite her age, Sophie had a good recovery. I was once again charge nurse on the 7 to 3 shift the day after her surgery. Making rounds on all the patients in CCU, I decided to keep Sophie as my last patient to assess. Sophie got an A+ on her physical. Vital signs were stable, the dressing over her pacemaker site was dry and intact, and Sophie was awake, alert, and oriented. Jotting down my last note on her condition, the Lord gently nudged me, reminding me of my promise to tell Sophie that Jesus loves her and is her true Messiah. Placing my clipboard on the bed table I said, "Sophie, I need to talk to you about Jesus."

"Humph," she sarcastically said, as she crossed her arms across her chest. "He is nothing but a scoundrel."

I quickly responded, "Sophie, that's not true. The other night you were dying. While Dr. Adams worked on you to save your life, you screamed a horrible, eerie scream three different times. God spoke to me while you were screaming for the third time. God said, *Georgia, Sophie is being pulled into Hell.* I promised God that if He spared your life, I would talk to you about Jesus. Sophie, Jesus loves you and gave His life for you. Jesus is indeed YESHUA HA-MASHIACH. Jesus wants you to accept Him and know that He is the true Messiah. Sophie, will you accept Jesus as your Messiah?"

Immediately, Sophie sat up in bed and yelled, "Yes!" Taking Sophie's hands in mine, I said, "Sophie, repeat this prayer after me. Dear Lord Jesus." Without hesitation, Sophie responded, "Dear Lord Jesus. Forgive me of my sins. Come into my heart and never leave me. Thank You Jesus for accepting me just the way I am. I love You Jesus and I give myself to You. In JESUS' name AMEN and AMEN."

When Sophie said Amen, she let out a big sigh and slipped back in bed. Then, she did the sigh thing two more times and just laid there motionless. I really thought she kicked the bucket. Just as I was ready to yell for help, Sophie sat straight up in bed with a smile from ear to ear.

I questioned her as to what just happened. "Sophie, why did you just take three big sighs and fall back in bed?"

"Nurse Georgee, I have just been taken from the kingdom of darkness to the kingdom of light." Her countenance had completely changed. Instead of a stern-looking, 94-year-old opinionated woman, I was now looking into a face that radiated joy unspeakable.

Nurse Rachael, observing this episode, questioned Sophie. "Sophie, do you really know what you just prayed?"

Sitting erect in bed with shoulders back and eyes fastened on Nurse Rachael, Sophie said, "Yes I do. I just accepted Jesus Christ as my Lord and Savior." Sophie, our little 94-year-old Jewish patient, was sent home from CCU the next day. Sophie was admitted to CCU with a damaged physical heart and discharged home with a new spiritual heart. Praise the LORD!

Reflecting on this miracle, I realized something that I had not seen before. Sophie had screamed three different times. After she asked Jesus to come into her life, she sighed, breathing deeply three times. Isn't it amazing how God can change one's life? Sophie went from calling Jesus a scoundrel to calling Him her Messiah and Lord within minutes.

Meditating on this wonderful miracle, I came to realize that Sophie was ready to hear the gospel presentation because she knew I was telling her the truth. When I told her about her screaming and being pulled into Hell, I believe for the first time her spiritual eyes were being opened. Sophie did not tell anyone about her hell experience. Would you? Therefore, she had to realize that God had revealed it to me. Thus, she was willing to hear about Jesus, the Messiah, for the first time in her life.

How many times I marvel at God's love for us. Think about it. A 94-year-old, Jewish lady, calling Jesus a scoundrel! Yet, He loved her so much that He saved her life to give her another opportunity to receive Him as her Messiah. AWESOME!

My last name being Cohen has led me to study the thinking of Jewish people and their relationship to God. It seems that Jewish people believe that you are either Jewish or Christian. Therefore, all Gentiles are Christian. This means that Hitler would have been a Christian. Now I understand why a Jewish person becomes offended when you mention the name of Jesus. In their mind, a Christian by the name of Hitler killed six million Jews. Thus, we understand why Sophie called Jesus a scoundrel. It usually takes a long time for a Jewish person to understand that not all Gentiles are Christian.

When I told Sophie that Jesus is indeed the true Messiah, He is YESHUA HA-MASHIACH, she knew exactly what I was saying. In Hebrew, YESHUA means to rescue or to deliver. YESHUA HA-MASHIACH is indeed GOD THE SON, THE PROMISED ONE, and THE REDEEMER OF ISRAEL and all mankind.

In the gospel of John, chapter 3 verse 16, we read: "For God so loved the world that He gave His one and only Son, that whoever believes in Him shall not perish but have eternal life."

Sophie chose to believe. I didn't know how many more years Sophie would have on this earth. But I did know that at the time Sophie took her last breath here she would immediately be in the arms of her YESHUA HA-MASHIACH. I can't wait to meet Sophie in heaven. Maybe she will greet me at the Pearly Gates.

CHAPTER 11
POPPY – MY JEWISH FATHER-IN-LAW

My father-in-law, who we lovingly called Poppy, was Jewish. Poppy was a wonderful man who accepted me, a Gentile, as his daughter-in-law. There was never a time in our relationship that I was ever ostracized. Immediately from the get-go, I loved Poppy and I knew that he loved me. He accepted me unconditionally as his only son's wife.

After my life was turned inside out and upside down when I received Jesus into my heart, I was excited about sharing my discovery with my family.

Poppy always responded, "George, leave me alone. I was born a Jew and I will die a Jew."

"Poppy, I would never attempt to take your Jewish heritage away from you. Of course you are Jewish. You will die with your Jewish heritage. But Poppy, I also want you to die as a Jew with Jesus."

It took years for Poppy to understand that he could still be a Jew and a Christian at the same time. His eyes were opened when he realized that not all Gentiles are Christian.

The hospital became Poppy's second home in his later years. Uncontrolled atrial fibrillation caused him to pay frequent visits to the hospital. The resulting poor circulation caused Poppy severe pain in his legs, taking its toll on his frail, emaciated body. I can still see him sitting in his favorite chair, rubbing his legs, hoping to get relief from the pain of this enemy. As if this wasn't enough, Poppy was diagnosed with Leukemia. More testing was needed to assist his doctor in his treatment. This cycle never seemed to end. Seeing Poppy's health in a constant downward spiral concerned me. *Was Poppy going to die only as a Jew, without Jesus? No, I will not give up.* Daily I prayed and presented my Poppy before the throne of God. Every opportunity I had, I tried to explain to Poppy why he needed Jesus as his Savior. In my eyes, it seemed that my words were falling on deaf ears. However, God was working. Poppy's grandchildren played a significant role in ministering to him. I don't think a day went by without the children telling Poppy that he needed Jesus.

Seven months before Poppy passed away, he was once again admitted to the coronary care unit. While Bill and I were preparing to go to the hospital to visit Poppy, our daughter Ginger stated that she needed to stay home and catch up on her school work. This proved to be very strategic. Our son Scott and daughter Colette joined us as we once again drove the familiar road to the hospital. Poppy's greeting was less than cordial. Upon entering his room, Poppy spewed out words of anger and frustration toward me. "George! You and your God! Look at me. My heart's a mess, I look like a skeleton, the pain in my legs is driving me crazy, and now they tell me I have Leukemia. I think I am dying. George . . . where is your God?"

Poppy's venting went on for a few minutes, followed by complete silence as we all stood around his bed. Breaking this uncomfortable period of silence, I said to Poppy, "Poppy, I don't know what else to tell you. I have shared everything I know about God with you. Poppy, you need Jesus."

Again, a long period of silence followed. This time Poppy broke the silence. Slowly turning his head toward me, Poppy said, "George, what do I need to do?"

Taking Poppy's hand in mine, I asked him if he was ready to totally surrender his life to Jesus.

"Yes, George, I am ready." WOW! There just aren't words to explain the joy that flooded my soul. My heart was pounding so hard and fast that I was sure it would burst. Holding Poppy's hands as we circled his bed, we prayed silently. Then I asked Poppy to repeat a simple prayer after me. He asked Jesus to forgive him of his sins and to come into his heart. The prayer ended with Poppy telling Jesus that he loved Him and thanked Him for forgiving him. When Poppy said Amen, he glowed with the biggest smile I have ever seen on his face. We immediately called Ginger at home and shared the good news. It was then that Ginger informed us that she called a friend to pray with her for her Poppy's salvation. Strategically, at the same time Poppy was ranting and raving about his illness and God, our daughter Ginger and her friend were praying for Poppy to surrender his life to Jesus. God hears and listens to the prayers of children. Ginger's prayer got God's attention, and He answered. What a joyous day that was! Poppy met God face to face and would never be the same. Every doctor, nurse, aide, dietitian, lab technician, and custodian heard Poppy talk about the love of Jesus and their need for Him as their Savior. Poppy lived another seven months before going to glory. Those seven months were the best months of his life. I can't wait to see Poppy in heaven! He's probably on the clean-up crew. Every time he came to our home he ran the vacuum sweeper. I'm sure the Pearly Gates will be shining and spotless on my arrival.

Somehow people seem to know when the end of their life is near. I don't pretend to understand this. However, I find it interesting. Never be afraid to offer a relationship with Jesus to a patient at this time in their life. Many patients over the years have said goodbye to me, telling me that they would die sometime before I would return the next day. For years, I always said stupid things in response to their statement, like trying to talk them out of their confession they just made. Me, the nurse telling my patients that they are doing better and need not think about death. Meanwhile, that is exactly what they wanted to talk about. I have finally come to realize that when someone tells me that they are dying, I take them seriously. These circumstances are a good time to listen to the patients and offer them the love of God. Remember the thief on the cross. He said to Christ, "Remember me." I try to never be too busy to spend time with a patient who expresses that they may be passing soon. It is probably their last opportunity to invite Jesus into their heart before going to glory.

Listen. Listen. Listen to your patients, family, friends, and the man on the bus.

CAN I GET A WITNESS?

CHAPTER 12
POLICEMAN & NEIGHBOR PETE

Pete and Carol were long-time neighbors. Carol would frequently invite me to her home, requesting prayer for her husband or children. Pete always got up out of his chair and left the room when I came to their house. He was always very cordial; however, he was not interested in being prayed for. I remember one time in particular when Pete had been quite ill. When I walked into their home, Carol called to Pete as he was quickly exiting the living room, "Pete . . . she's a good pray-e-r." Pete was nowhere to be found. Prayer for the macho policeman was out of the question. Carol had come to the saving knowledge of Jesus Christ and longed for Pete to have this same experience.

Accepting Jesus into your heart is a very personal experience. You can't push, beg, bargain, manipulate, or shout Jesus into another's being. Prayer is the best thing you can do for your loved one. God loves them even more than we do. Be a good, loving Christian and let the Holy Spirit do His work.

It was 10:30 P.M. when the phone rang. It was Carol. "Georgia, Pete is in Mercy Hospital. He was diagnosed with cancer of the lungs, which has just spread to his brain. The doctor said he is losing blood and just had a stroke. They are giving him blood transfusions. Georgia, Pete is scared. He just called me from the hospital and said, 'Carol . . . I need Georgia.'"

Excitement filled my being. Pete didn't need me. He needed Jesus. I'm just the messenger. I told Carol I would go early in the morning to see Pete.

Visiting patients early in the morning seems to be a good time. Nurses are getting ready for report, and the chaos of the day has not yet started. A calm, quiet atmosphere prevails at this time. It was still dark as I pulled into the Mercy Hospital parking garage at 5:30 A.M. Pete was sitting up in bed, with eyes wide open, looking like a deer facing headlights. Upon entering his room Pete said, "Georgia, I'm dying."

I immediately responded and said, "Pete, have I got good news for you."

"You do?" Pete exclaimed.

Gently taking Pete's hand in mine, I softly spoke to him about heaven. "Pete, do you realize that this life on earth isn't our true home?"

"Why no," Pete responded. "What do you mean?"

"While living on earth we are living in temporary housing. We are just passing through. Our real home, our permanent home, is in heaven with Jesus. Pete, in the Bible, in John 14:1-3, Jesus said:

> 'Do not let your hearts be troubled. You believe in God, believe also in me. My Father's house has many rooms; if that were not so, would I have told you that I am going there to prepare a place for you? And if I go and prepare a place for you, I will come back and take you to be with me that you also may be where I am.'"

Pete, Jesus is preparing a special place in Heaven for you right now."

Pete yelled with all the strength he could muster, "WOW! It sounds like we can't lose."

"That's right, Pete. Jesus loves you, Pete, and wants to have a relationship with you. If this sounds like something you desire, we could pray right now."

"Georgia, I don't know how to pray."

"Pete, that's O.K. I can pray, and you can say the prayer after me."

"That sounds good to me, Georgia. Let's give it a go."

"Dear Lord Jesus."

Pete's weak, quivering voice responded immediately, "Dear Lord Jesus. It's Pete, the policeman. Forgive me of my sins. Thank You, Jesus for forgiving me, and for being so patient with me over the years. I am sorry it took me so long to come to You. I invite You into my heart. I give myself to You. Thank you, Lord, for accepting me just the way I am. I love You, Jesus. Amen!"

When Pete finished his prayer, a heavenly glow radiated from his countenance. Pete, looking at me with eyes wide open said, "Glory be to God." In a matter of minutes, Pete's dead spiritual being came to life. Pete lived on this earth for ten more days. Every time I came into his presence, Pete radiated with the love of God.

Listening! Listening to the voice of God is the only way to witness. Upon entering Pete's room, I had no idea what I would say. Plus, I didn't know that Pete was going to tell me he was dying. God knew what he would say. God knows our thoughts before we even think them. God is in control. When we listen to Him, He always makes a way. God will give us the right words to say at the right time. We need to be obedient and go where He wants us to go and be the witnesses He has called us to be. God is saying,

CAN I GET A WITNESS!

CHAPTER 13
MAX (AKA MR. ELEPHANT)

The Medical Strategic Network (METS) conducts conferences throughout the United States and internationally. The purpose of these five-day conferences is to equip believers with the knowledge of giving sound spiritual care to patients. The grand finale of the METS conference is when the participants in the conference take part in a practicum conducted at various hospitals. This is the time to put into practice what has been taught during the conference.

My husband Bill and I had just finished attending our first METS conference in California. Hospital assignments were handed out for the practicum. The METS equipped us with Spiritual Care Questions to ask patients. We were told that the patients knew we were coming. With excitement and feelings of intimidation, we were off and running. After gathering together in the hospital lobby for last-minute instructions and prayer, teams of two were sent to various hospital units. Bill and I paused for a brief moment of prayer outside the room of our first patient. Just before entering the patient's room, I glanced at the patient's name. The last name was Elephant. I took a second glance. His last name indeed was Elephant. I couldn't believe it. How would I get through the questions calling my patient Mr. Elephant? So, I decided to sophisticate his name. Introducing myself and Bill, I called the patient Mr. El – a – font, you know, something like the French might say.

Sitting, dangling on the side of his bed, the patient was very annoyed at me. "Elephant! Elephant!" he yelled, "Just like the animal. It's not El – a – font."

"Maybe we could go on a first-name basis, what do you think?" Glancing at my sheet of names given me by METS, I saw his first name was Archie. "May I call you Archie?"

"My friends call me Max."

"May I call you Max?"

"Yeah, go ahead."

"Then, Max it will be." I was mystified concerning Max's angry demeanor. I reasoned that perhaps Max didn't know we were coming. Maybe he felt we were intruding on his privacy. Regardless of my bumbling efforts of introduction, Max was not a happy camper. Should I offer an apology for him not knowing that we would be coming? Yet we were told our assigned patients were asked ahead of time if they wanted to participate in the spiritual assessment practicum. "Max, did you not know that we were coming today?"

"Oh yes," Max immediately replied with a big grin on his face. "I have been waiting for you."

Wonderful! They didn't cover mean, angry, Sumo-looking wrestlers in the METS conference. Now what do I do?

Gently and ever so softly God spoke to me. *You just do it. Ask the questions from the spiritual care questionnaire and leave the rest to Me.*

With fear and trepidation, holding the Spiritual Care Assessment in my hand, I slowly began asking Max the first question. "Max, how long have you been in the hospital?"

In the meanest, loudest voice Max could muster he replied, "FIVE DAYS."

"Question number two: How has it been going for you?"

"Peachy," was his sarcastic answer.

"O.K. Question number three! What has been your source of strength during your illness?"

Yelling like one might, at an Army and Navy football game; Max, glared at me and said; "Groceries and good beer!"

I started to chuckle at Max's response. I couldn't help it. He was trying his best to get me upset. Yet God, in His infinite mercy, poured buckets of His love on me to transfer onto Max. I remember standing up, looking Max in the eye, placing my hand on his left shoulder saying, "Max, I really like you." The angrier Max became, the more love I felt for him. It was crazy. This insulting, angry frame of a Sumo man spewing out crude insults at me during the questionnaire was the same man that I was loving to pieces with the love of God. I think I was more surprised by this display of love than Max was. "Can we go on to question number four?"

"Yeah," he yelled.

Maybe he thought I was hard of hearing. Whatever! "Max, where has God been during your illness?"

"NOWHERE," Max exclaimed.

Not knowing what to do or say, I continued on. "Question five. What has your illness done to your relationship with God?"

Max, now sheepishly grinning, almost laughing said, "It's been great. He leaves me alone and I leave Him alone."

I was at a dead end, going nowhere fast. Putting the questions aside, I took a pamphlet out of my pocket. Holding it so that Max could see it, I asked Max if we could go over it together. "Max, it talks about having a relationship with God. Would you like to read it with me?"

"No," he immediately responded.

I then placed it on his table and said, "Maybe later you might be interested in reading it."

"No, I don't want it."

I quietly stood praying silently for Max. *Wisdom, Lord, I need your wisdom and guidance.* Placing my hand on his left shoulder, I asked Max about his life. "You must have had a hard life, Max. I see some pain and sorrow. Tell me about it."

Max sat shaking his head, looking out the window with glazed eyes. "Yeah."

"Max, what happened? Let's talk about it."

Max just sat there. The silence seemed to never end. His body language now transformed from the former Sumo wrestler to tear-filled eyes. With his head on his chest, almost unable to speak, Max quietly uttered, "During the war, we were in the heat of the battle. My buddy and I were hiding in a fox hole. When my buddy knelt and prayed, he was shot to death." Moments of silence passed.

"Max, what else happened to you?"

"My mother suffered with cancer and died."

God filled my mouth, and I responded. "Did your mother hate God?"

"Oh no," Max immediately replied. "My mother loved God and prayed all the time."

"Help me understand something, Max. You are not facing imminent death, right?"

"Right," Max said.

"But you are mad at God?"

"You got that right."

"Max, your mother suffered with a lot of pain and died with cancer, yet she didn't hate God but loved God and prayed all the time?"

"Yeah, that's right," Max replied, sitting bent over with his head resting on his chest.

Taking the Spiritual Care pamphlet in my hand, bending over to get eye contact with Max, I said, "Max, for the sake of your mother's prayers, would you read the pamphlet?"

Max slowly sat erect in bed, eyes wide open, looking straight at me. A period of silence lingered throughout this staring contest. Max broke the silence stuttering; "Yes, for the sake of my mother's prayers, I will read your pamphlet." Taking the pamphlet in both hands, Max pulled it to his chest, holding it tight. As tears slowly dropped from his eyes, Max asked me if I would pray for him.

Listening to God is the key to sharing the love of God with others. The Holy Spirit will tell you what to say as you rely on Him for your guidance. Every situation is different. Remember, you are just the messenger or witness. You can't save anyone. Be yourself, love others unconditionally as God has loved you, and leave the results up to the Holy Spirit. Giving a testimony as to what Jesus has done in your life is being a witness for God. Failing to witness is when we refuse to open our mouth and say, "Look what the Lord has done!"

A successful witness is one who testifies about our Lord and Savior Jesus Christ. Whether a person receives or rejects the good news about Jesus does not reflect your performance as a witness. Our Lord commanded us to go and tell others about Him. We don't save anyone, anyway. That is the Holy Spirit's job. If we don't go and tell, then who will? Be obedient. Open your mouth as the Lord leads, and shout it from the house tops that Jesus Christ is Lord.

God is looking for a witness. Will you be His witness? Will you be an Isaiah and go where He wants you to go and do what He wants you to do? Ask yourself: Am I willing to be used by God? Am I really willing to be used? I thought I was willing; however, when the opportunity to witness would come along, I became the good silent witness, which is no witness at all. I've shed tears of regret, but God has forgiven me for refusing to open my mouth in situations He laid before me. We are good at justifying our speechless actions. I became an expert at it. Finally, when I became serious about being His witness, I was able to be obedient. Wasting years of my Christian life, never telling anyone about Jesus, I regret my silence.

Witnessing is a way of life. A baby must learn to crawl before he can stand. No matter how many times a baby falls when trying to stand, he never gives up. Through tears, bumps, and bruises, a baby is determined to one day stand on his own. Eventually, the day comes when the little one is able to do it. Baby pulls, pushes, grunts, groans and voila, is standing. Joy and laughter overwhelm the baby. Overcome with his laughter, he of course falls flat on his bum. Is he discouraged? No. Not at all! Hey! He now knows he can stand. Immediately, he tries again. Without much exertion he finds himself standing stronger than ever. Taking a step is now his next hurdle. Does a baby stop? Never! You get the picture. We are babies when it comes to witnessing. The key is to start. You may fail many times. That's O.K. Eventually; you will stand tall, like our baby. Then you will take your first step. Before you know it, you will be off and running.

There is no greater joy than telling others about the love of our precious Savior, Jesus Christ. That love is to know that Jesus gave His life, died, and rose again so that we could live our life forever with Him.

CAN I GET A WITNESS?

CHAPTER 14
NO! NO! - I'VE SEEN TOO MUCH

Ken, a 78-year-old male, was admitted to CCU with the diagnosis of myocardial infarction (MI), AKA a heart attack. Ken's recovery period had been uneventful. His vital signs were stable throughout his stay in CCU. The morphine drip had been effective in eliminating his chest pain. After seventy-two hours, all lab results were now within normal limits and Ken was pain-free and off the morphine drip. It was time for Ken to be transferred out of CCU.

Introducing myself to Ken, I gave him the good news that he was well enough to be transferred. While assisting Ken with packing up his belongings, I felt very strongly that the Lord was leading me to talk to Ken about God. "Ken, may I ask you a question?"

"Sure."

"Where was God during your heart attack and your stay here in CCU?"

"What do you mean?"

"Did you sense that God was with you during these past few days?"

"Oh, now I understand. No, I don't believe in God and I don't want to have anything to do with Him."

"Ken, why don't you believe in God?"

"I've seen too much. I've just seen too much and now I am old."

"May, I explore this with you?"

"NO! Nurse Georgee, there is nothing you can say that would ever change my mind. I have seen too much."

I felt so helpless. My words of how God loved him just the way he was fell on deaf ears. Ken shut the door to God, and it would never be opened. In my spirit, I felt like I was begging him to give God a chance. I have never felt so compelled to share the gospel. Ken was very polite and not argumentative. He just had no use for God.

Ken was well enough to be transferred in a wheel chair with a portable monitor attached to his body recording his heart rate and rhythm. During the transfer, we made small talk, laughed about a couple of things, and talked about going home in a few days. His new room on the tenth floor of the hospital was bright and welcoming. After unpacking his belongings and introducing him to his new nurse, I said my goodbyes and returned to CCU.

One hour later a Blue Alert (emergency call) was heard over the PA system of the hospital for the tenth floor. Over and over, the PA system rang out the words Blue Alert, Blue Alert tenth floor. My heart sank. Could it be Ken? Was he okay? Was he alive? My mind was bombarded with unanswered questions. My break would be in forty-five minutes. I could go to Ken's room and see if he was okay. I knew that I couldn't just call the nurse's station and ask questions about a patient that was no longer mine. Those forty-five minutes seemed like forty-five hours. Finally, the time arrived. Notifying the nursing staff that I was now going on break, I made a bee line for the tenth floor. I decided to take the steps instead of the elevator. Briskly walking down the corridor on the tenth floor, I noticed that the door to Ken's room was closed. Slowly, pushing the door ajar, I saw an empty bed, stripped of its linens. It was Ken's bed. The Blue Alert was Ken. He didn't make it. Ken died! Ken died! Closing the door to Ken's room, I sat in his chair and cried. I couldn't believe that Ken was dead. Medically speaking, Ken was stable.

God, You knew. You knew time was short. That is why I felt so compelled to talk with Ken about his relationship with

You. Help me Lord to always be obedient to your guidance and leading when it comes to witnessing. Father, You know best. I love You, Daddy.

CHAPTER 15
EYES LIKE DIAMONDS

The Old Stone Church, on the corner of the village square, commanded the attention of everyone passing by. Majestic in structure, yet small in capacity, it was the landmark and point of reference for directions to our town. Capacity in the sanctuary was only two hundred and fifty, making it easy to spot a new face on a Sunday morning.

It was a typical December, Sunday morning. The Christmas tree was richly decorated, standing at attention in the foyer. Christmas carols were playing in the background as the congregation gathered in the sanctuary for the 10 A.M. service. Approaching the tenth row from the altar, where we always sat, I noticed a visitor sitting at the end of the row. Greetings and introductions were made. I couldn't help but notice that our visitor, Grace, appeared a little glum. Looking closer, I noticed that her face was stained with tears. When the service ended, I invited Grace to join me for breakfast. The rest is history.

Grace was sixty years old. Her husband passed away two weeks prior to our meeting. Bill and I adopted Grace into our immediate family. Two months later, Grace invited Jesus into her heart, asking God to forgive her of all her sins. Grace became a new creation in Christ. She radiated with the love of God. It was wonderful seeing Grace as our most enthusiastic greeter on Sunday mornings.

In October of the following year, Grace was diagnosed with breast cancer, requiring a radical mastectomy. Grace was a trooper. Her recuperation period went well. Grace looked lovely as she greeted people for our Thanksgiving service. In December, I noticed that Grace had a tint of jaundice. She mentioned to me that she wasn't feeling quite right for the past week. After many tests, Grace received the bad news. The cancer now had invaded her liver. Grace's life quickly ebbed away. Within a week, Grace lapsed into a coma, totally unresponsive to any verbal commands. During my frequent hospital visits, I asked Grace to open her eyes and squeeze my hand. There was never a response. Grace's nieces and nephews were diligent at staying by her bedside at night. I offered to relieve them so they could get a good night of sleep. I told them I would be there as a friend, not as a nurse. We all agreed. My turn with Grace was Friday night. With my Bible and Methodist Hymnal in hand, I went to visit Grace. I was excited to be alone with Grace in her private room. Throughout the night, walking around her room and holding her hand while sitting beside her, I sang hymns, read scripture out loud to Grace, and prayed. Of course there was no response from Grace. However, that did not stop me from ministering to her. I believe that Grace heard every word I uttered. At 4:00 A.M. I decided to sit at the foot of her bed and read scripture. All of a sudden, Grace sat straight up in bed. This woman that couldn't even squeeze my hand was now sitting erect in bed. I couldn't believe it. Jumping to my feet, I yelled, Grace. . .e. . . .e. . . .e, Grace. . .e. . .e. . .! Looking intently into Grace's eyes, I felt like she was looking right through me. I remember turning around to see if someone else was present. I didn't see anyone. I was dumbfounded. I just kept yelling Grace. Then I noticed her eyes. They had been totally dis-colored due to the jaundice. The whites of her eyes were an ugly yellow. Now, with Grace sitting totally erect in bed, I noticed that the whites of her eyes were absolutely a brilliant white. Her eyes were sparkling like diamonds. They were beautiful, magnificent, radiant, and absolutely lovely. Standing there speechless, I was trying to understand what was happening. Grace then closed her eyes, and very gently lay back in bed. She was gone. No pulse, no heartbeat, no respirations. Grace died. Yet, what just took place?

This totally unresponsive woman sat up in bed with eyes wide open. I believe Grace saw Jesus. Only JESUS could change ugly, jaundiced eyes to diamonds. Jesus escorted Grace to her heavenly home, to be with Him forever. I can't wait to see you Grace.

CHAPTER 16
I WANT TO DONATE
MY ORGANS

It was another typical day at the office, so Bill thought. While on his coffee break, Bill collapsed to the floor. His coworkers immediately started CPR and called 911. The medics intubated Bill, started IVs, and connected him to a monitor and external defibrillator. The medics called our CCU notifying us that they were on their way. Within twenty-five minutes, Bill was admitted to CCU with the diagnosis of cardiogenic shock. This is an extremely serious condition in which the organs in the body are not receiving an adequate circulation of blood to keep them functioning. Cardiogenic shock is caused by the failure of the heart to pump effectively; thus, a patient has sustained low blood pressure, resulting in the body shutting down. Death of the patient is imminent.

Bill was assigned to me. I notified his cardiologist and the resident on call. Standing at attention at the entrance to Bill's room, I greeted the medics and Bill. I was ready and prepared. Surprisingly, Bill was completely awake, alert, and oriented. However, he had to write to communicate with me, since he had the endotracheal tube in his mouth with the ventilator attached, breathing for him.

After introducing myself, I asked Bill if he knew Jesus as his Savior. I am not usually this abrupt; however, I knew medically speaking Bill was at death's door. Bill aggressively shook his head in affirmation that he knew Jesus, folding his hands to pray. Cupping my hands around Bill's, I prayed and asked the Lord to bless him and give him peace. Informing Bill that his family had been notified of his admittance to CCU, I continued with my assessment. Dr. Scott and his resident arrived and inserted an arterial line to measure his blood pressure. We could not obtain a blood pressure with a cuff because his blood pressure was too low for the machine to calculate it. Only a catheter, placed in Bill's femoral artery, connected to the monitor in his room, would record his true blood pressure. After successful insertion of the femoral catheter, his blood pressure was recorded at a systolic of 34. This reading is not enough to sustain life. Dr. Scott ordered IV pressors in an attempt to raise Bill's blood pressure. All IV medications were wide open, running as fast as possible in an effort to raise his blood pressure. Nothing worked. Bill's systolic blood pressure remained in the low 30s. It seemed hopeless. I was praying for the Lord to keep Bill alive until his family arrived so they could see him one last time. My prayer was abruptly interrupted by God with a reprimand.

Georgia, get your eyes off of the medical equipment and onto the spiritual realm. I want you to take authority over the spirit of death in Bill's room now!

Not having the faith to believe that Bill could possibly survive, I decided to discuss this situation with the Lord. *God, I don't think it is appropriate for me to pray like that in front of Bill. I know he is going to die, and You know he is going to die. If I go in his room and start taking authority over the spirit of death, then Bill will know he is dying. I don't want to scare him to death. I am praying he will live to see his family one more time.*

God was not interested in what I had to say or my opinion. He was relentless, commanding me to do what He told me to do. Finally, I succumbed to his leading. Slowly walking into Bill's room, I closed his door and pulled the curtain shut. Of course, my eyes were on the call light to make sure no one was listening in. *I am trying to be obedient Lord, but isn't there a limit? I thought yelling the sinner's prayer in the Burn Unit was bad enough. I have never taken authority over the spirit of death. What will Bill think? What if he gets scared and reports me? What if I lose my job? How will I explain my lack of employment to my husband? He will have me committed.* God was totally unimpressed with my wailings. Over and over and over again, I heard God tell me what to do as I stood motionless at Bill's bedside. *God, I prayed, You have to give me the boldness to do this. I am so scared. Help me to be obedient and listen to You. Okay, here it goes.* "Bill, I need to pray for you again." Bill shook his head in agreement. "Bill, my prayer is a heavy-duty prayer that God is asking me to do." Again, Bill shook his head in approval. I encouraged Bill and MYSELF with the words of God in the Bible. "You know, Bill, that nothing is impossible with God. He can do anything." Again, Bill shook his head in agreement. "Okay Bill, let's pray. In the name of Jesus, every knee will bow and every tongue will confess that Jesus Christ is Lord. That means that you, foul spirit of death, must bow your knee to my Jesus. Therefore, I am taking authority over you, foul spirit of death, in the name of Jesus Christ. My God came to give Bill life and life more abundantly. Bill, be healed in the name of JESUS. AMEN!"

Taking a deep breath, I pulled open the curtain, opened the door, and slowly walked to the nurse's station. My heart was pounding so loud, hard, and fast, I was sure someone would hear it. I sat down in front of the monitors and just about passed out. Everyone was oblivious to me or what just happened. I was shaking like a leaf, but I must admit, that I was quietly praising God that I was obedient to the call. Medically speaking, nothing appeared to change. Bill's blood pressure continued to hover in the 30's. Bill remained awake, alert, and oriented. All IVs were still running wide open. It is times like this that we must keep our eyes on Jesus, the author and finisher of our faith.

Bill's family eventually arrived. Dr. Scott advised them to notify all family members that Bill would probably die tonight if not sooner. Bill's wife, Mary, was very concerned about finding exactly where their son, Butch, lived. They knew he was living in a trailer park in Georgia. Mary said Butch didn't have a phone, so she didn't know how they could reach him to tell him his dad was dying. I called the local police and informed them of our problem. Mary gave them Butch's address. They said they would contact the Georgia police and have them stop by Butch's trailer. Mary confided in me that Bill and Butch had not talked to each other in over ten years. Bill apparently had wanted to have reconciliation: however, Butch was never ready. I prayed with Mary that God would keep Bill alive long enough for Butch to get here to see his dad.

Within two hours, all of Bill's family, except Butch, was gathered in the CCU waiting room. After greeting them, I offered to pray for them. We received word that the Georgia police located Butch. He was able to book a flight and would be arriving in at midnight. Again, I prayed with the family that God would keep Bill alive until his son could see him.

At 9:00 P.M., Mary informed me that Bill always wanted to donate his organs when he died. I immediately called Mrs. Fuller, our nursing supervisor, informing her of the family's request. When all the legal papers were signed, I called the organ donor bank. They asked me a ton of questions, about Bill's condition. The process took about thirty-five minutes.

Finally, Betty, the donor bank representative replied; "I have bad news." What? What could possibly be wrong now? Betty told me that Bill was just about dead since his organs couldn't possibly be receiving enough blood to sustain them; therefore, his organs were of no use to them.

Great! I can't even offer the family a little solace in their time of despair. They want to do something good, and I have to tell them they can't do it. *I don't believe it. God, what is going on?* Just as I was ready to end this conversation with Betty, she told me that they could use his eyes, if the family was willing to donate them when he dies. Well, I thought, I guess that is better than nothing. I informed Mary of the decision the donor bank made and explained to her why they couldn't take his organs. She said she would talk to the rest of the family about his eyes and let me know. I notified Mrs. Fuller of the results as well.

The time was now 10:30 P.M. I still had to get ready for report and wrap things up. At 11:45 P.M., I said my goodbyes to Mary and her family. Driving home, I felt consumed with everything that happened. My sleep was frequently interrupted with me praying for Bill and Butch to reconcile and for the family to make the right decision about Bill's eyes.

I decided to go into work a little early the next day. I was anxious to get all the details about Bill and his family. Did his son Butch arrive O. K? Did the family finally come to a decision about Bill's eyes? Just as I was ready to push those big CCU doors open, Nurse Carol was coming out.

"Georgia!" she shouted. "Bill's alive! He made a complete recovery in the middle of the night. Apparently, last night after his son Butch visited, Bill rebounded. His blood pressure and all his vital signs returned to normal. Georgia, he's healed!"

I was so excited. I ran to his room. Bill was sitting up in bed, watching TV. He looked fantastic. Bill and I grabbed hands and cried. *Oh, God, I prayed. Thank You for healing Bill. We know this is a miracle. You are the healer of all our diseases. God, forgive me for not having the faith to believe. You are awesome, God. Help my unbelief.* I was overcome with joy unspeakable. I just couldn't believe it. Bill, medically speaking, should not be alive. What a miracle! "Bill, how did things go with your son last night? With tears running down his cheeks, Bill nodded, as he reached for his pen and paper. "All is well, Nurse Georgee. All is well." "Thank you, Jesus!" I shouted. It was time for report, so I told Bill I had to go.

Bill was transferred to a regular floor the next day. No ventilator, monitor, IVs, Swan-Ganz catheter or arterial line! Dr. Scott gave Bill a clean bill of health. When the nurse on Bill's floor was making her evening rounds, she offered Bill a sleeping pill. He politely refused and asked for his prayers instead. The nurse seemed a little confused, not knowing what to do. Bill advised her to call CCU and ask for me.

When Agnes, his nurse, called, she stuttered a little, when asking me if I pray with my patients. Yes, I do pray with my patients. How may I help you? She informed me that Bill is waiting for his prayers and she didn't know what to do. I told her I would be right down.

Bill was so glad to see me. "Nurse Georgee, they don't know what I am talking about when I asked for my prayers."

"That's O.K., Bill. I will explain it to Agnes."

It was a wonderful opportunity to witness to his new nurses. I shared the miracle of Bill's healing and why he wanted his prayers. Bill knew that he was alive, only because of his risen Savior. He was ready to tell the world about his healing.

Two weeks later, Mrs. Fuller returned from her vacation. Her last night at work was when I called her concerning donating Bill's organs. While making her hospital rounds, Mrs. Fuller asked me whatever happened about Bill, the patient in room 32, and did the family decide to donate his eyes. "NO, they decided he needed them," I said. Then I explained the marvelous miracle that took place. To God be the glory. Not only did God heal Bill physically, but he granted him a healing in his relationship with his son. My God is so awesome! *I love You Lord. Forgive me for my unbelief.*

CHAPTER 17
HELLS ANGELS VERSUS THE OUTLAWS

Fear permeated the CCU that cold, December morning. During report, we were advised that we would be receiving a prisoner from the Federal Penitentiary at 9 A.M. All chart documents on this prisoner were extremely confidential. Of course, this is true of every patient admitted to a hospital. However, this patient, Oscar, was very different. Our hospital would not have his name on the admission record. In CCU, his chart would not be in the routine chart bin. His chart would be in an unmarked envelope in a locked cabinet. Why all the fuss? Our prisoner, Oscar, was a member of the motorcycle gang called the Outlaws.

The hospital top brass along with the police attended report that day. This was a first. The police were very specific in their instructions regarding the admission of Oscar. We received a crash course in motorcycle gangs. The Outlaws and another motorcycle gang called Hell's Angels are enemies. Each of these gangs would stop at nothing to annihilate each other. Therefore, the secrecy of Oscar's admission to CCU must be carried out. The police informed us that if the Hell's Angels were aware that Oscar was in CCU, they would charge the unit and kill Oscar. No one in the hospital, except CCU nurses, would be aware of Oscar's admission.

It was difficult to remain focused on caring for the other patients in CCU while waiting for Oscar's arrival. Every single time those big doors flung open to CCU, every nurse froze in their tracks. Was Oscar here? The hour from 8 to 9 A.M. was overwhelming, with routine visits from doctors; supervisors; lab, EKG, X-ray technicians; and dieticians. Fear mounted with every opening of the doors to CCU.

At 8:45 A.M., we followed strict orders to pull the curtains and close the doors to each patient's room. I tried to remain calm while waiting for our new patient. At 9 A.M. sharp, the doors again flung open with a bang. Oscar arrived with his police escort and medics. While transferring Oscar from the stretcher to his bed in CCU, I was startled at the site of handcuffs on his wrists. The reality of the seriousness of Oscar's admission to CCU hit me like a ton of bricks. Just as I regained my composure, the policeman accompanying Oscar, attached the handcuffs around Oscar's wrist to his bedframe. I stood there with my mouth open in disbelief. Oscar's arms were stretched down along the bed so the handcuffs could be securely attached to the metal bedframe. He looked so uncomfortable. It seemed so cruel to treat another human being in this manner, especially while he was suffering from chest pain during his heart attack. The policeman was without expression as he took his seat at Oscar's bedside. Oscar would be handcuffed with a policeman at his bedside throughout his hospital stay. The rest of the day was pretty much a blur. In nurses training, they didn't cover caring for prisoners with policemen in attendance, charts with no names, and handcuffs. This was a whole new ball game.

Rehearsing the day's activities caused me to toss and turn throughout the night. During my drive to work, I prayed for the Lord to give me peace of mind and strength for the day. Oscar was not assigned to me as a patient. I must admit that I found myself rejoicing that I did not have to deal with this exhausting situation. However, Oscar put his call light on while I was outside of his room. There was no way that I could ignore his call light if I was standing right outside his door. I had to go in his room and attend to his request for more pain medication. While increasing his morphine drip, I tried to make small talk. "Oscar, what do the Outlaws do?"

Grunting, and slowly speaking, Oscar said, "They kill people."

Well, that was all I needed to hear. Fear overwhelmed me as I quickly left his room. I immediately started to pray that the Lord would make sure that I would never have to take care of Oscar. My mind was racing with absurd thoughts. I just couldn't handle this situation. God is so good. I never did have to take care of Oscar. His time in CCU was uneventful. Three days later, Oscar's condition was stable. He and the policeman were transferred to a step-down unit. I rejoiced. My rejoicing lasted fifteen minutes. All of a sudden, I felt the Lord impressing me to interact with Oscar.

Lord, what do You mean? You want me to go and visit him in his new unit? Unbelievable! Finally, when things can get back to normal in CCU, You want me to go to Oscar and have a chat? WHY?

Georgia, I want you to take a Bible to him. It must be the NIV version. Tomorrow when you go to work, you are to give him this Bible and tell him I still love him.

Okay, Lord. I will do it.

It just so happens that I just purchased a new NIV Bible the previous week. All of a sudden, I was enveloped in complete peace. The fear was gone. I actually felt excitement about seeing Oscar the next day. I was given an assignment, and by George, I would do it.

Excitement filled the air as I drove to work the next morning with my NIV Bible. I just couldn't believe what the Lord did in my life. All fear was now gone and unspeakable love and compassion for Oscar filled my soul. *God*, I prayed. *I will go where You want me to go and I will do what You want me to do.* Arriving forty-five minutes early, I had plenty of time to visit with Oscar. With my NIV Bible tucked under my arm, I gallantly marched to Oscar's new room. After greeting the policeman, I informed him that he could go on break. I instructed him to remove the handcuffs and leave the room for thirty minutes. It never occurred to me to have the handcuffs removed and to have the policeman leave the room. It just happened. I was a little surprised myself when I boldly spoke these words to the policeman. Yet, I had such a peace that I never gave it a second thought. "Oscar, God spoke to me last night and told me to bring you this NIV Bible and to tell you that He still loves you."

Oscar started to cry. I couldn't believe it. This big hunk of a motorcycle man was crying. Wiping the tears from his eyes, he informed me that he had accepted Jesus as his Savior years before. Then, as life happens, he fell away from the Lord and did his own thing. While in prison, his grandma sent him the NIV Bible. He loved his grandma and treasured her gift to him. Before coming to the hospital, he asked if he could take his Bible with him. The answer was no. "Georgia, I have felt so lonely. How I longed to have my Bible with me. Now I know that Jesus really does care about me."

"Oscar, Jesus is crazy about you. We are going to have church. Come on. Sit up on the side of the bed." We read scriptures, sang hymns, and worshiped the Lord of lords and the King of kings. Oh how glorious our time together was. We had just finished when the policeman came back. "Well Oscar, it's time for me to go. Oscar, don't ever forget what Jesus said. He will never leave you or forsake you. God Bless you, Oscar."

As I walked out of Oscar's room, I heard the sound of the handcuffs click shut around Oscar's wrists. Yes Lord! Oscar is one of the prisoners you have set free. Handcuffs on the outside; but freedom and peace on the inside. Hallelujah!

CHAPTER 18
I'M A CATHOLIC

Nunzio was admitted to CCU with end-stage cardiomyopathy. This condition eventually necessitates the need for a heart transplant. Due to weakness of the heart muscle, the heart markedly enlarges, which in turn affects the ability of the heart to pump effectively. The result leaves a patient gasping for breath with the slightest exertion.

My pastor called and informed me that Mary's dad, Nunzio, had been admitted to my hospital. Mary was a member of our congregation for years; however, I never had the opportunity of meeting her dad. "Georgia, would you please visit him and pray for him? At present, I am feeling a bit overwhelmed and overcommitted. I am unable to get to the hospital at this time. My schedule is completely booked until 10:00 P.M. tonight with meetings and appointments, and tomorrow I leave for a conference in California for three days. I understand Nunzio is quite ill. A visit to encourage him would be wonderful. Tell him that I will visit him in about a week if he is still in the hospital."

"Pastor, I would be happy to visit him. I have been off for a couple days and am well rested. I will go in early tonight so I can spend time with Nunzio before I start my shift. I will give you a call after my visit, informing you of his status. Have a safe and informative trip. I will keep you in my prayers."

"Thanks Georgia. Look forward to your call."

Arriving at the hospital forty-five minutes before my shift, I had plenty of time to visit Nunzio. Glancing at the patient assignment for the night, I saw that Nunzio was not assigned to me as one of my patients. It's a good thing I came in early to visit him. Once the assignments are made they are never changed. If a patient is not assigned to you, you mind your own business. A nurse can answer another patient's call light; however, that is the extent that you interact with a patient that has not been assigned to you. You never tread on another nurse's territory.

Nunzio was admitted to room 36. With thirty minutes to spare before my shift began, I entered Nunzio's room. "Hi, Nunzio. My name is Nurse Georgee. Pastor Tom asked me to pay you a visit. So, how long have you been going to East End Church?"

With his big, brown glaring eyes staring a hole through me, Nunzio said, "I AM A CATHOLIC. I don't go to your church. My daughter goes to your church."

"I am so sorry. I assumed you went there. We have several services on Sunday and Saturday night; it is hard to know everyone with a congregation of 3000 members. Please forgive me. I'll see you later." And with that, I ran out of his room. Boy, did I blow that one. How could I have been so stupid? I never meant to offend Nunzio. Oh well, it's water over the dam. *Lord, please forgive me and send someone else to pray for Nunzio. Maybe I could call the hospital priest to follow up.* We were so busy that night with blue alerts and new admissions that I completely forgot about Nunzio and my blunder. Nunzio was history, or so I thought.

When I reported to work the next day at 3 P.M., I was told that the CCU step-down unit needed help and that I would be working there. A nurse has to be flexible and willing to adjust to any and every situation. Nurses grow attached to their unit and inwardly resist going or being pulled to another unit. So be it! It was my turn to be pulled, and I had to go. After reporting to the step-down unit, I was given my assignment of six patients. Two hours later, my assessments, charting, and treatments were done. I was caught up with nothing to do. I noticed that Audrey was frantically running around like a chicken with its head cut off. I asked her to let me help and asked what I could do to lighten her patient load.

"I don't know, Georgia. I am so overwhelmed."

"Please Audrey, I am caught up. What do you need? Do you have patient assessments you want me to do? Maybe you have some dressing changes or IV lines that need changed. Whatever! I am willing to help."

"Well, I could really use your help with a patient that needs his dressings changed. They take a while to do and are rather extensive. Are you sure you don't mind?"

"Of course not, what is the patient's name and what room is he in?"

"The patient is in room 8243 and his name is Nunzio." I couldn't believe it. *Lord, this is really funny. I guess You want me to finish what I started yesterday. Well, no turning back now. I just begged Audrey to let me help her with her patients. I didn't even know that they had transferred Nunzio to the step-down unit. Lord, give me wisdom and discernment and favor with Nunzio. This has to be a divine appointment. Let's get started.*

Just before I walked into Nunzio's room, I shot up another prayer for help. I must admit I walked into his room with my tail between my legs. "Hi Nunzio, I am Nurse Georgee. I will be helping you tonight with whatever you need."

He shook his head in agreement and closed his eyes. Standing at the foot of his bed, I looked at Nunzio for the first time. He looked so helpless. His body filled with fluid made him look like the Dough Boys' brother. His dinner tray sat untouched on his bed table. His arms were so swollen that it was impossible for him to maneuver enough to feed himself. Compassion overwhelmed me for this very sick patient.

"Nunzio, I need to change the dressings on your legs, but first I would like to reheat your dinner and assist you with it. Is that O.K.?"

"Yes Nurse Georgee, that's fine."

After helping Nunzio sit more erect in bed, I propped pillows under each arm to help support his breathing. While slowly feeding him, I made small talk and then said, "Nunzio, all my life I went to church. What about you? Have you always gone to church?"

"Oh yes. My parents made sure we were in church every Sunday." "What is the name of your church?"

"It is St. Mary's of the Mount."

"Wow, that's a big church."

"Did your parents go there?"

"No, they went to St. Elizabeth in Brownsville. That's where we lived when I was growing up. My parents are buried in the graveyard in the back of that church."

"Isn't it wonderful to have a family tradition of church going when growing up?"

"Yep, it sure is. I miss that old church. But, it's too far to travel. It's over three hours away from where I now live."

"I miss my old Methodist Church too. All my friends were also at the church. We even had a bowling alley in the basement. We sure had a great time. But now we go to East End Church since it is much closer to where we live."

"Nunzio, it looks like we both have a great heritage."

"Nurse Georgee, I think you are right."

Surprisingly, Nunzio ate most of his dinner. As I unwrapped the dressings on his legs I said, "Nunzio, even though I went to church all my life, I never understood what it meant to have a relationship with Jesus and to be born-again. It took me thirty-two years before I understood this born-again stuff. What about you? Since you went to church all your life, can you explain to me what it means to accept Jesus as your Savior and to be born-again?"

"No Nurse Georgee, I never did understand it. My daughter Mary has tried to talk to me about it. I just don't get it."

"Nunzio, may I try to explain to you what it means to be born-again?"

"Sure."

I proceeded to share my personal testimony with Nunzio. "I had so many questions about life in general that never seemed to get answered. I wanted to know: why, was I here and what was life all about? Even though I went to church all my life, I had no peace. I felt unloved, lonely and depressed. I never heard my parents say they loved me. I longed to be loved and accepted. My sister, Barbara, became born-again. She seemed so happy. Every time she saw me she told me that I needed to ask Jesus into my heart and to ask Him to forgive me of my sins. The funny thing is that I didn't think that I had any sin. I never killed anyone. I always tried to be kind to my neighbors. But as Barbara put it, everyone has sinned, and what do you do with the sin? Barbara said you give it to Jesus. Finally, the day came when I stopped running from God. I got down on my knees and called out to God. I asked Jesus if He would come and live His life in me. I asked Him if He would take my sins and forgive me for all my wrongs. I realized that fighting with my mother-in-law, among other things, was a sin. All of a sudden, I felt a fantastic peace throughout my body. I never felt anything like that before. It felt like a thousand pounds fell off my shoulders. I called my sister and told Barbara what happened, to which she replied, 'Georgia, YOU ARE SAVED. YOU ARE BORN-AGAIN.' I couldn't believe it. It was so easy. All I had to do was ask Jesus to take my sins away, forgive me, and come and live His life in me. WOW! God answered my prayer. After years of running from God, He didn't run from me when I finally bowed my knee to Him. Instead, He embraced me in His ever-loving arms and said He would never leave me or forsake me."

Putting the last piece of tape over Nunzio's new dressing I said, "Well, Nunzio, what do you think? Are you ready to be born-again and ask Jesus to forgive you of your sins?"

"Yes, Nurse Georgee, I believe I am ready, but I am not sure what I am to do."

"Nunzio, you just talk to God like you are talking to me."

"Will you help me if I get stuck?"

"I'm here for you. Let's give it a go."

"O.K. God, it's me, Nunzio. My Nurse Georgee said I need to ask You to forgive me of my sins. God, I am sorry for the way I have treated people. I have been so mean. Please forgive me and help me to be nicer. Jesus, would You come into my body and live in me and show me how to live? Forgive me for getting mad at my daughter Mary when she tried to talk to me about You. Nurse Georgee, should I say anything else?"

"You might want to thank Him for Mary and for loving you and accepting you just the way you are."

"Oh, that's good. Yes, I will do that. Jesus, I do thank You for my daughter, Mary, and for You loving me just the way I am. AMEN!"

Just as Nunzio said amen, Audrey came in the room to see how we were doing. She thanked me for helping her to catch up with all her treatments. She appeared much calmer and so did Nunzio.

God, You are so good. Everything is in your perfect timing. You never cease to amaze me in the way You always orchestrate every detail and direction in our lives. If only we would listen to You and not always insist on going our own way. God, forgive me for being so bull-headed

CHAPTER 19
GRANDMA'S CROSS

S tacy was admitted to CCU with complaints of shortness of breath and heart palpitations. These symptoms had increased in intensity over the previous few days, necessitating admission to the hospital. Stacy, sixty-three years old, lived with her parents and sister in a little town called West Booten. Blind since birth, Stacy became overly dependent on her family for support. This was her first hospitalization, causing her great anxiety and fear. Reassurance was given to her and her family that we would be diligent in always being available for her comfort and support.

Stacy was my patient. On admission, I realized how scared and intimidated she really was. Being separated from her family for the first time in sixty-three years was overwhelming. Orienting her and her family to CCU, I tied the call light to the bed rail and put the call button in her hand. I also told Stacy that if she ever lost her call button, all she had to do was yell. "Stacy, our nurse's station is right outside your room. Someone is always close by. You don't have to worry. We will never leave you alone. Just give us a holler and we will be there."

Four hours later, Stacy was starting to stabilize and appeared to be resting comfortably. Her medications were working, and she was on the mend.

On my next rounds I found Stacy resting comfortably, listening to the TV. While checking her vital signs, IVs, and urine output, I asked; "Stacy, has anyone told you about the peace you receive when you accept Jesus as your Savior?"

"Nurse Georgee, I'm not sure what you are talking about. My parents do take me to church every Sunday. I like going to church and I like my Sunday school teacher. They are so kind to me. You said something about Jesus and peace. What do you mean?"

"Stacy, do you know what it means to have a personal relationship with Jesus?"

"I'm not sure that I do. Does going to church every Sunday and to Sunday school mean that I have a relationship with Jesus?"

"I suppose that it would mean that you have somewhat of a relationship with God. I guess a good analogy would be if you always go to the local grocery store every Monday and talk to the owner of that store. You greet the owner, buy your groceries, and go home. You do this every Monday of every week of every year. Do you have a relationship with the owner of the grocery store? Do you know where he lives, if he has a family or any pets, or what kind of car he drives? What time does he get up and when does he go to bed? So, my question to you Stacy is: what kind of a relationship do you have with the owner of the grocery store?"

"Well, if you put it that way, I guess I would have to say it is a very distant relationship. I really don't know anything about him. I greet him every Monday, and never think about him the rest of the week. I only know his name."

"Now, let's get back to Jesus. Would you say that your relationship with Jesus is the same as the relationship you have with the owner of your grocery store?"

"You know what? I think you are right, Nurse Georgee. I never thought about it before. I guess I really don't know Jesus very well."

"Stacy, you can have a personal relationship with Jesus, every second of the day. He wants to talk with you and He wants you to talk to Him. What do you think?"

"How does that happen? What do I need to do?"

"Stacy, a personal relationship with Jesus starts when you ask Jesus to forgive you of your sins. And you know what? Not only does He forgive you of your sins, but He even forgets your sins. He holds nothing against you. The slate is clean. Then you invite

Jesus into your life and into your heart. Jesus always accepts your invitation. He will come into your heart and never, never leave you. What do you think about that?"

"Wow! Now that's a relationship that I want. Can we pray now?"

"Sure. Stacy, talk to God just like you talk to me. Ask Him to forgive you of your sins, thank Him for forgiving you, and then invite Him into your heart."

"O.K. here it goes. Jesus, I am sorry I never knew You. I thought I was a Christian because I always went to church and Sunday school. Now I understand that I never really knew You. I knew about You, but never had a relationship with You. Nurse Georgee said I could have a relationship with You; that I could talk to You and You would talk to me. Jesus, forgive me of my sins. I invite You into my heart. Please don't leave me. Thank You for being my friend and for forgiving me of my sins. Amen. Nurse Georgee, was that prayer O.K.?"

"You bet your bottom dollar it was. Your prayer touched heaven and God heard you. Stacy, you are now a Christian, you are born-again, and Jesus will never leave you. Promise me that you will talk to Him every day. Jesus loves you Stacy."

"Oh I will talk to Jesus every day. Thank you so much for teaching me how to have a relationship with God. It is awesome." I said goodnight to Stacy and told her I would see her tomorrow.

Driving home, I basked in the glory of God. I was so happy for Stacy. Rejoicing over my conversation with Stacy, I felt the Lord nudging me in a direction I didn't want to go. Yet, His persistence was overbearing. *Are you sure Lord? You want me to give Stacy my grandma's pearl cross necklace? She made it for me. I never thought about giving my necklace to anyone. It means a lot to me. Every time I wear her pearl cross necklace, it brings back memories of our times together. God, I know that I shouldn't cling to the things of this world, but my grandma's necklace. Why?* God never answered me. He continued impressing upon me that I needed to give my grandma's pearl cross necklace to Stacy, and that was that. O.K. *Lord. You win. I don't understand, but I know that You have everything under control. I will take the necklace to work tomorrow and give it to Stacy.*

Arriving at the hospital thirty-five minutes before my shift, I made a beeline to CCU. I must admit that I was excited to see Stacy, even though I wasn't thrilled about giving grandma's necklace away. Stacy had stabilized enough to be transferred out of CCU to a monitored step-down bed. She was now on the third floor of the hospital. I took the steps instead of the elevator to the third floor. Our elevators were not the fastest, and the clock was ticking. Entering her room, I found Stacy sitting erect in bed and wide awake. "Hi Stacy, it is Nurse Georgee from CCU. How are you doing?"

"Not so good."

"Stacy, what's wrong?"

"I couldn't sleep last night. I'm scared, Nurse Georgee. I saw the devil sitting at the bottom of my bed, laughing at me. He kept laughing and laughing. What is going to happen to me? I don't know what to do."

Compassion for my little blind Stacy overwhelmed me. I got so mad at the devil. How dare he torment my little blind lady? "Stacy, Jesus will take care of that devil. I want to read you something from the Bible. In the book of James, chapter 4 verse 7, it reads, "Submit yourselves; then, to God. Resist the devil, and he will flee from you." Stacy, yesterday you submitted yourself to Jesus when you prayed and accepted Him as your Lord and Savior. Do you remember that?"

"Oh yes, Nurse Georgee. I will never forget it."

"Okay, then. You and I are submitted to Jesus. We did what the Bible said. Now we just resist the devil and he has to go. I will now pray and you believe with me, O.K.?"

"Yes, I'm ready."

"Dear Jesus, I know that all things are possible with You. I thank You, that You have given me authority over the enemy. In Jesus' name, I plead the blood of Christ Jesus over Stacy. In the name of Jesus Christ, I take authority over you, Satan, and command you to get out of this room and never torment Stacy again. Jesus has set her free and you cannot torment her. She is protected by the blood of Jesus Christ. Thank You Jesus that You have set Stacy free and that no weapon formed against her can prosper. We love You Jesus and pray this prayer in Your precious name. AMEN and AMEN!"

"Stacy, it is done. The devil is gone and you have been set free."

"I feel so much better. I feel like a new person."

"Stacy, God spoke to me yesterday on my way home from work. He told me to bring you the pearl cross necklace my grandma made for me. Now I understand why." Taking grandma's necklace in my hands, I slowly placed it over Stacy's head and around her neck. It laid beautifully displayed on top of her nightgown. Grandma's necklace never looked so good. Then I took Stacy's hand and placed the pearl cross in her palm, closing her fingers tightly around the cross. "Stacy, anytime you feel afraid, you just need to remember the cross, hold it in the palm of your hand, and call on Jesus. He is always there for you." Smiling from ear to ear, Stacy absolutely radiated with the joy of the Lord. "I need to get to work. God Bless you, Stacy. I probably won't see you again. I assume the doctor will let you go home today. It was wonderful meeting you." Bending over her bedrail, I kissed her radiating face goodbye, taking one last glance at grandma's cross.

Oh, grandma, if you only knew what your pearl cross necklace did for a little blind lady. *God, You are so good and I love You. Sorry it takes me a while to be obedient. Sorry for all the questions I ask. Thanks for being patient with me.*

CHAPTER 20
BIG MAC ATTACKS

I couldn't believe what I had just overheard Dr. Charity say to one of my patients. How cruel! Just plain rude and tasteless and without any compassion! Righteous anger was oozing out of every pore in my being. Standing in the door way to Don's room, in a stupor of disbelief, Dr. Charity brushed me aside as he bull-dozed his way to the nurse's station.

Looking at Don while walking into his room, I saw a patient with no hope. Sitting in his bed with his head down on his chest and arms folded, I noted a few tears on his cheeks. "Don, my name is Nurse Georgee. I will be taking care of you today. I overheard what your cardiologist, Dr. Charity, said to you. I am here to offer you hope and a future."

"What hope could you possibly offer me? You heard what the doctor said. Dr. Charity said I am nothing but a dead man. If I have the surgery, he said I will die on the operating room table. If I don't have the surgery, I will die. I am nothing but a dead man without hope. Oh nurse Georgee, I can't believe it. I survived my heart attack and thought I was on the road to recovery. I tried not to eat many hamburgers at McDonalds. I only had one Big Mac every other week. I have really tried to watch my diet. And now, with this rhythm problem, there is no hope for me. I'm only 48 years old. I have two little boys at home. Are they going to grow up without a dad? What about my wife? She is so dependent on me. How can you come in here and tell me you can offer me hope when my doctor said I'm a dead man? That's not very funny."

Silence followed Don's comments. Don finally lifted his head and looked at me. "Don, if it is O.K. with you, I would like to share where I get my hope for today and my future."

"What have I got to lose? Sure, go ahead."

"Don, my hope and my trust is in God."

"GOD! Wow! Now we're going to get religious. Nurse Georgee, I don't even go to church anymore. I don't know what I believe. How can God give me hope if the doctor said there is no hope?"

"Don, my hope is in God alone. My hope is not in money, doctors, nice cars, or mansions, only God. May I proceed to share with you my relationship with God?"

"Okay."

"Don, eleven years ago I was despondent, suicidal, and totally hopeless. I didn't want to live anymore. Feeling unloved and hopeless, I was ready to pack it up and call it a day. Then in the middle of my despair, I met Jesus. Don, Jesus loves me and He loves you. I got down on my knees and invited Jesus into my heart, asking Him to forgive me of my sins. Immediately, I was enveloped in a warm cloud of God's love. It was amazing. I never felt like that in my entire life. Not only did God love me and bathe me in His love; He gave me love for those I didn't love because of the way they treated me. It was amazing. Don, God can and will give you hope for tomorrow. Nothing is impossible with Him."

"Nurse Georgee, I believe every word you said. You know why I believe you? Because you told me what you believe. You didn't tell me what Billy Graham, Oral Roberts or Robert Schuler believes. You told me what you believe, and I want to believe like that too."

"That's great Don. The first step is to invite Jesus into your heart. Jesus promises to never leave you or forsake you. He is always just a prayer away. After you open up your heart to Jesus, and invite Him in, you need to ask Him to forgive you of your sins. He promises to forgive and forget all our sins and to cleanse us completely."

"Wow! That is good news! Nurse Georgee, there's just one problem. I've never prayed before. What do I do?"

"Don, I will lead us in prayer. You can repeat after me what I pray. Is that O.K.?"

"Sounds good!"

"Dear Lord Jesus. It's Don praying. Please forgive me of all my sins. Thank You for forgiving me. Come into my heart. Thank You that You will never leave me. I love You Jesus. Amen!" "Don, you did it. Jesus is in your heart and He loves you just the way you are. Talk to Him every day. He loves to hear from His children. Praying to God is just talking to Him, just the way we are talking. You don't need fancy words to talk to God. You don't need to be a priest or a minister to talk to God. He is anxiously waiting to hear your prayers."

"Now Don, I think it is time for me to pray for you. Let's ask God for His direction for your life. Is that O.K.?"

"That would be great. I want you to pray for me."

"God I thank You for Don's salvation. Bless him with Your peace that is beyond all understanding. Give him hope. Dear Lord, reveal clearly to Don what he should do! Should he have the surgery or should he forget about it? Lord, I ask that You heal him of this chaotic heart rhythm. Let Don know if his healing will come through the surgery or without the surgery. I place Don in the palms of Your majestic hands. Thank You, Jesus, for answering our prayers. We love You Jesus. Amen."

"Don, you can tell me later what you decide about your surgery. Remember, God is with you in whatever decision you make. Your doctor does not have the final word. The buck stops with Jesus, not the doctor. Never forget that."

Don rested quietly over the next two hours. His vital signs remained consistent with his chaotic rhythm on the monitor. He was stable in his unstable condition. Just before lunch, Don put his call light on. "Nurse Georgee, I'm going to have the surgery. I have decided to trust Jesus. I know He is with me. My life is in His hands. Bring the papers in and I will sign them. I actually have peace about my surgery. I can't believe it. Thank you so much for helping me to understand that God is in control and not Doctor Charity."

"You are welcome Don."

Don had his surgery the next day. His surgeon put an AICD (automatic implantable cardiac defibrillator) in his chest. If Don's heart rhythm raced to a level that would not sustain life, his AICD would fire and his heart would be restored to a normal sinus rhythm. Don had a successful surgery without any complications. He was discharged home the day after his surgery. We received a letter from Don two weeks after his discharge. It was so cute. He thanked all the nurses for taking care of him. He said he was doing well with only one problem. He was still having **BIG MAC ATTACKS**.

CHAPTER 21
I'M AN EPISCOPALIAN

Isolation patients can be very time-consuming. They are totally isolated from other patients and all nursing staff, with their door closed and curtains pulled 24/7. Their diagnosis necessitates this type of environment for their protection as well as the protection of others, including visitors and all hospital staff. Thus, the isolated patient is often lonely, discouraged, and depressed. Their hospital room is secluded and separated from all the hospital activity. They are living in a world surrounded by silence. This is why I would always spend extra time with my isolation patients. Their contact with the outside world is limited, with few visitors. Once my nursing assessment was completed, I always spent time in conversation, discussing any concerns they might have.

Reviewing my assignment, I would then decide the order in which I would assess each patient. My isolation patient was always last. This way I knew that my other patients would be okay while I was behind closed doors.

It was a very busy Tuesday morning. One patient after another was having a cardiac arrest, and I was assigned the isolation patient. The harder I tried to catch up, the further behind I got. Finally, my two unstable patients stabilized to the point that would allow me to leave them for a brief period. Our step-down unit sent one of their nurses to relieve me long enough so I could assess our isolation patient. I had just finished washing my hands putting on my gown, mask, and gloves when I heard my nurse manager calling me. "Georgia. Telephone." Great! I was irritated that I had to take a phone call. I was behind in my assessments and the clock kept ticking away. Would I ever get caught up with all these unnecessary interruptions? As my nurse manager impatiently waved the phone receiver in the air, waiting for me to take the call, I marched into the nurse's station in my big "yellow bird" outfit. I had just wasted a few minutes getting ready to assess Harry, my isolation patient, and now I would have to re-gown and do it all over again. If I walked around in the same gown I would wear into Harry's room, I would be carrying all the CCU germs into his presence. I would have to re-gown. Would I ever be caught up? Grabbing the receiver from my nurse manager's hand, with the phone cord extended from the desk between two doctors trying to chart and a nurse's station filled with people and commotion I said, "This is Georgia, may I help you?"

The quivering voice on the telephone quickly got my attention. "Georgia, this is Marge, Harry's wife. How is he?" Not waiting for my response, she just kept talking. "I'm an invalid. I can't get in to see Harry. I miss him so much. I haven't been out of my house for five years. Harry always does everything for me. I hope he is O.K. Georgia, I have four sons and one of them is a minister. He is born-again. Of course, I am not born-again because I am an Episcopalian." Silence followed; she just stopped talking. I finally got my mind off of my troubles of running behind and concentrated on this little old invalid lady.

"Marge, do you know that Episcopalians can be born-again."

"Why, No! I didn't know that."

"Yes, Marge. Everyone can be born-again. It doesn't matter what religion you are. Jesus wants to have a relationship with you, regardless of what religion or church you go to. Would you like me to explain more to you about being born-again?"

"Oh, Georgia, yes, please tell me more. I just don't get it." I became oblivious to the doctors charting, all the people in the nurse's station, and the ticking clock. This was a divine appointment and I needed to seize the moment. Briefly I shared with Marge that we are all sinners since birth. The only way to cleanse ourselves from our sin is to give the sin to Jesus. Jesus forgives us of our sins and then He forgets our sins; they are gone. We get to start over again. It is kind of like being born all over again; a fresh start on life. We now have a spiritual relationship with God. Our once-dead spirit jumps to life when we ask Jesus to come into our lives and forgive us of our sins. "Marge, does what I said make sense to you?"

"YES, YES it does." Marge was so excited. She kept yelling, "I understand, I understand, it is a matter of belief!"

"Honey, truer words have not been spoken. You are right. There was a man in the Bible that asked Jesus to help him with his unbelief."

"Georgia, I'm not sure how to ask Jesus to forgive me of my sins. Can you help me?"

"Absolutely Marge, I will lead you in prayer. You repeat the words after me. Are you ready?"

"Yes, Georgia, I am ready." I had her repeat the prayer after me. "Dear Lord Jesus. Forgive me of my sins. Thank You for forgiving me. Come into my heart and live Your life through me. I love You Jesus and I thank You for loving and forgiving me. In Jesus' name Amen."

"Marge, now you know that you are born-again."

"Thank you so much for taking your time to help me understand this. I will call my minister son and tell him that I am now born-again, just like him. But Georgia, wait a minute. I am concerned about Harry. He isn't born-again. He's an Episcopalian too."

"Marge, I am going into his room now. I will tell him about our conversation. Who knows? Maybe he will also want to be born-again."

Harry was a very sick, unstable patient. He suffered from a cardiac arrest with many complications. He now presented with MRSA (methicillin-resistant Staphylococcus aureus) pneumonia, congestive heart failure, and frequent episodes of irregular heart rhythm. He was alert and oriented despite all complications and being on a ventilator. After doing Harry's assessment, I talked with him about my conversation with his wife. He was very interested and communicated with me by writing. Harry said that if Episcopalians could be born-again, he was ready to be like his son the minister. Harry prayed a prayer to receive Jesus into his heart. When he said "Amen," his face radiated with joy unspeakable. He asked me to call his wife and inform her that he has joined her in being born-again, just like their son.

Things eventually quieted down in the unit that day. Our patients stabilized and we were able to get caught up with all the charting. Driving home, I was wrapped in the Lord's presence. *Thank You, Lord, for Marge and Harry. I realized that Marge's contact with the outside world was very limited. This indeed was a Divine appointment. In the middle of asking about Harry, she threw into the mix that she was not born-again. I was so preoc-cupied with the ticking clock and having to re-gown that I almost missed what You were doing. Help me Lord to slow down and to always be mindful of Your presence, even when time is slipping quickly away. By the way Lord, thank You for the unnecessary interruptions.*

CHAPTER 22
HE'S IN MY HEART

Excitement and anticipation filled the air while driving to Florida Hospital in Orlando. The METS Whole Person Care Conference just completed several days of training in giving spiritual care. Now it was time to put into practice what we learned. All the METS participants gathered in the Florida Hospital auditorium waiting for our last-minute instructions. Chaplain Bob was our leader at the hospital. Dividing us into groups of four, Chaplain Bob gave each group their patient assignment. After prayer, we were off to see our patients. The goal was to put into practice the spiritual care that had just been taught over the last three days.

I gathered my team together for prayer before entering the patient's room. Each team member would have the opportunity to visit with at least two patients depending on the time. My team was professional and courteous. We finished our patient assignment quicker than normal due to the discharges on our list. I called Chaplain Bob for more patients. We were off again to another unit. Time was ticking and we needed to meet in the auditorium at 4:30 P.M. One patient was left. It was Sandi on the rehabilitation unit. We inquired at the nurse's station where we might find Sandi. The nurse manager told us she was in the recreation room. After offering a brief prayer before entering the room, I told Jackie that she would be the one to talk with Sandi. Jackie nodded her head and said, "O.K., but if there are family members with Sandi, I can't do it."

"Let's just trust God and see what happens," I told her.

There were only two people in the recreation room. They were playing Scrabble. Sandi and her son were so engrossed in the game that our presence went unnoticed. Elbowing Jackie to make introductions, I noticed her perspiring and looking a little peaked. I took the lead and made introductions. Then I told them that Jackie would be the one doing the questionnaire. By this time she had herself together and did quite well.

Sandi proved to be a challenge. After Jackie explained about the questionnaire, Sandi said she didn't want to do it. Burt, her son, spoke up and said, "Mother, you told them you would participate. You need to keep your word."

"I don't have my glasses. I can't do it." Before we knew it, Burt was up and running to her room to fetch them. This did not make Sandi happy. She told Burt that he was trying to distract her so she would lose at Scrabble. Taking her glasses, she had no choice but to do what her son expected her to do.

Jackie was now relaxed and ready to proceed with the questionnaire. Sandi pushed the Scrabble board aside and was polite and attentive to Jackie as she asked her the spiritual questions. Sandi was totally absorbed in participating in the questionnaire. When Jackie asked the last question, Sandi asked, "Aren't there any more questions?" Jackie then introduced a tract presenting a clear presentation of the Gospel. Sandi was very eager to explore the booklet. With her glasses now securely in place, Sandi read the booklet out loud, while Jackie sat by her side

Sandi was totally engrossed in the booklet. After Jackie went through the first few pages of the booklet, she asked Sandi if she was ready to have a relationship with God. Sandi, holding onto the booklet for dear life, excitedly said "YES."

Jackie turned to a prayer at the back of the booklet. "Sandi, would you read this sample prayer and tell me if this sounds like something you want to do."

"Jackie; yes, I want to know Jesus. What comes next?"

"Sandi, read the prayer out loud with all your heart. The prayer is a way for you to surrender your life to Jesus. If you are ready, we will silently be praying as you pray."

Sandi, sitting erect, held the booklet firmly in her hand. She pronounced each word clearly while praying the prayer. Her voice started quivering and a few tears stained her wrinkled 95-year-old face. Sandi, reverently prayed the sample prayer in the booklet and received Jesus as her personal Savior. Burt then could no longer hold back his emotions. Covering his face with his arms, leaning over the Scrabble table, Burt cried like a baby. I also at this point lost it and began to shed tears. The atmosphere in the recreation room was a heavenly bliss. This little old lady who just wanted to play Scrabble with her son was now praying and accepting Jesus Christ to be her Savior. It was awesome.

When Sandi was finished praying the prayer in the booklet, Jackie asked her where was Jesus now. Placing her right hand over her chest, she said in a crackling, high-pitched voice; "He's-s-s in my heart."

Tears of joy exploded in the recreation room. Burt then informed us that he has witnessed to his mother for years. Burt lived in Florida, and Sandi lived in Montana. While visiting her son, she fell and received several bruises. Thankfully, she didn't experience any broken bones. His doctor thought it best for her to spend a day or two in the rehabilitation unit until she was more stable.

Isn't God absolutely amazing? He brought a 95-year-old mother from Montana, over 2,000 miles away, to visit her son in Florida. Circumstances were such that she wound up in the hospital, only to have a METS team come in to her recreation room to share with her the love of Jesus Christ. Oh, what a SAVIOR.

The icing on the cake was when we found out that it was her birthday. I took the METS team to the cafeteria, where we were able to get a birthday cake. Then we went to the hospital gift shop. We found a coffee mug filled with candy. The mug had kisses on it with the words LOVE YOU WITH ALL MY HEART written all over it. When we arrived back at the recreation room, we were surprised to find it full of visitors. I made an announcement that today was Sandi's birthday. Everyone joined in singing "Happy Birthday" to our new born-again, 95-year-old mother from Montana.

CHAPTER 23
LOOK FOR THE SPIRITUAL DIAGNOSIS

In every conversation we engage in, our mind should always be focused on looking for a spiritual diagnosis. When an individual does not know Jesus as their Savior, they are spiritually sick. They need medicine to treat their illness. The medicine to cure spiritual sickness is the Bible. They need to meet the Great Physician, the best diagnostician in the world. Jesus is the Great Physician and has the cure for every spiritual disease.

Before I surrendered my life to Christ, my spiritual disease was hopelessness. My sister, Barbara, encouraged me, daily saying, "There's a better way Georgia, and His name is Jesus." I knew the way I was going was disastrous. Barbara treated my hopeless spiritual disease with the hope we have in Jesus Christ.

We are all doctors for Jesus. Good doctors always do a complete history and physical on their patients, leaving no stone unturned. In our daily encounters, we also need to do complete assessments when talking with others. As Christians, we need to do a spiritual assessment on every person we come in contact with. The goal of the spiritual assessment is to diagnosis the spiritual problem. Once you pinpoint the problem, you have your spiritual diagnosis. The treatment for the spiritual diagnosis is the word of God. The Bible is God's penicillin for the human race.

I saw Ruthie as a mean, sarcastic, troublemaker. Jesus saw a precious young lady in need of knowing that she was loved. Ruthie's spiritual diagnosis was feeling unwanted, uncared for, friendless, unvalued, rejected, unwelcomed, shunned, spurned, neglected, and abandoned. The treatment was the love of God. Ruthie cried when she read the words on her cake: "You are loved."

I saw Amos as a man afraid of someone messing with his heart. His spiritual diagnosis was fear. When I prayed for God to help him with his decision, his fear left and the healing began. Through the constant reinforcement of God's love for him during his time in CCU, my final conversation with Amos led him to ask Jesus into his life. Amos at this point became ripe fruit. He was ready to receive what God had for him. There was no arm twisting or coercing. Amos was ready; just as a peach on a tree falls gently into your hand when ripe; Amos fell gently into the hands of The Almighty God.

Big John displayed his doubt about salvation. "Georgia, I just don't know about this Jesus." He talked to me about his life and how he wanted to change it. Fighting and beating people up was a thing of the past. Guilt over his behavior consumed him. How could God forgive him for what he had done? His spiritual diagnosis was doubt in God and guilt. The treatment was God's love.

Sophie was face to face with hell. Her spiritual diagnosis was fear of dying. The treatment was the truth of the gospel. When confronted with the truth that Jesus was her true Messiah, her fear had to go.

Poppy was caught up in his Jewish heritage and that it couldn't possibly include a Gentile Jesus. His spiritual diagnosis was doubt and unbelief. After years of witnessing to Poppy that Jesus loves him and is his true Messiah, Poppy finally invited Jesus into his heart. The treatment for Poppy was the truth of the gospel.

Pete presents with a spiritual diagnosis of a fear of dying. The treatment was in the Bible in John, chapter 14. Our hope in Christ gives us confidence that there is life after death.

Max was consumed with a spiritual diagnosis of anger towards God. The treatment was encouraging him to talk about the anger. God can take it.

In chapter sixteen we see a very sad man. Ken was cemented in his past of hurt and pain. He camped out there years ago and refused to move on. His spiritual diagnosis was un-forgiveness.

Oscar presented with a strong, arrogant, disposition. This proved to be a facade. God revealed to me that his spiritual diagnosis was doubt. Oscar doubted God's love. Surely, God didn't love and care for him anymore. In obedience to God's leading, Oscar was reconnected with his Savior when I gave him a Bible. The treatment for his diagnosis was the word of God.

Nunzio was just like Poppy and Sophie. He was caught up in a religion and not the person of Jesus Christ. His spiritual diagnosis was lack of truth. The treatment was a clear explanation of the message of salvation.

Don was filled with a fear of dying. His spiritual diagnosis was hopelessness. The treatment was my brief testimony of what the Lord has done for me.

Marge was confused about how she could be born-again, like her son the minister, even though she was an Episcopalian. She was also caught up in a religion without a personal relationship with the God of this universe. Her spiritual diagnosis was unbelief and lack of truth. The treatment was a short but clear presentation of the gospel.

Sandi was caught up in the moment of playing Scrabble with her son. Her spiritual diagnosis was lack of interest and no time for God. After all, it was her ninety-fifth birthday. How many more opportunities would she have to play Scrabble with her son? The treatment was God using her son to encourage her to comply with her promise.

In my encounters, as I search for the spiritual diagnosis, my mind is on witnessing. Jesus came to seek and save the lost. Shouldn't we do likewise? Trust God to fill your mind and mouth with each step you should take. As you search for the spiritual diagnosis, God will lead you to the path of treatment.

CHAPTER 24
THE BOTTOM LINE

Looking back at my time in CCU, I now realize that my City of Faith began when I bought Ruthie the cake. My pit of hell was simply a mirage. Freedom to pray with patients was granted. I was requested to go to other hospital units and pray for their patients. These requests were from nurses on those units. A compromise was made on the unit regarding the music on the radio in the nurse's station. We rotated radio stations. One day it was secular music, no longer hard rock, and the next day it was Christian music. Eventually, all swearing ceased and smoking became forbidden in CCU. Nurses made decisions to receive Jesus as their Savior. Many were transferred from CCU to other units in the hospital. Strategically, this was brilliant. When I was transferring a patient to the Cath lab, PCU, operating room, or a MED-SURG unit, I would phone ahead and talk with the Christian nurse on that unit. She would then welcome the transferred patient and pray for them. Patients were covered in prayer wherever they were sent in the hospital.

If I would have gone to City of Faith Hospital in Oklahoma, I would have missed out on what God wanted to do, right in my own home town. If I would have stepped out in front of the Lord and selfishly done my own thing, by uprooting my family and moving to what I thought was best, it would have been disastrous. Doctors and nurses who had worked in City of Faith Hospital informed me, years later, that they were not permitted to pray for patients. Patients at City of Faith were admitted with a prayer partner. It was the prayer partner only who had permission to pray with a patient. Yes, on each of my interviews, I was told that every patient was admitted with a prayer partner. Of course, I assumed that meant that there was freedom to pray with our patients. Foolish me! It wasn't until the doctors and nurses started to work at City of Faith that it was made clear that they were never to pray with patients. This was my heart's desire. If I would have done it my way, we would have sold our home, my husband would have quit his good job, our children would have missed their life-long friends, and we probably wouldn't have seen our Poppy again. The icing on the cake was, I would have been forbidden to pray with my patients. INCREDIBLE! Now, the second icing on the cake is this! City of Faith Hospital in Oklahoma actually closed. KAPUT! How do you like that? God knew all along what would happen. He actually protected me and then blessed me with my own City of Faith. What a wonderful Savior. I didn't need to know these details, at the time. God was looking for my OBEDIENCE to Him. That's all He ever wants. That's the bottom line.

CHAPTER 25
WITNESSING TIPS

1. **Listening is the key to witnessing.** Listen with your physical ears to what your patients are saying. Listen with your spiritual ears to where the Holy Spirit is leading.
2. Obedience is the next step in being a witness. When God opens a door for us to share the good news, we must obey and walk through the open door.
3. Give a gospel tract to your patients, friends, and people passing you on the street, on a bus or plane. Put tracts in your bills when you send them in for payment. Leave tracts at the gas pump, restrooms in restaurants, and with your tip at the end of your meal.
   a. Leaving a tract with a patient is absolutely the easiest way to introduce them to the gospel. Always ask permission to do so. Time is so precious, and we have little of it while working shifts in a hospital.
   b. When entering a patient's room, first take inventory. Look around and observe what the patient is watching on TV. What are they reading? Do you see a Bible?
   c. Just before leaving the patient's room, take a tract out of your pocket and say: "Mark, I have a little pamphlet that will encourage you in your faith. Would you like me to leave it for you to read when you get a chance? Perhaps after work

I could come back and we could discuss what you read." I have never had anyone refuse to take the tract. This is such an easy approach.

d. Your job is to find a tract that makes you feel comfortable. When you return after work, let the Holy Spirit lead you in your conversation.

e. You can contact Good News Publishers at <u>www.goodnewstracts.org</u>. Order a variety pack of gospel tracts. Read them and choose one that you are comfortable with. It is always good to choose one that has a prayer of salvation at the end.

f. If you would like to have a tract that leads you step by step in witnessing I suggest "Would You Like To Know God Personally?" You can purchase this tract at any Christian Book store, or write to Campus Crusade For Christ, Inc. The ISBN is 1-56399-018-0, published by New Life publications, a ministry of Campus Crusade For Christ. I always leave this tract with a patient, and if they prayed to accept Jesus as their Savior, I write the date and time they prayed in the tract.

g. Tracts especially good for teenagers are cartoon tracts. You can purchase these from Chick Publications at P.O. Box 3500, Ontario, Ca. 91761, or call 909-987-0771

h. Think of questions you could ask before you ever approach someone. The person's answers to your questions will help you know where they are spiritually. Your question helps lay the foundation for follow-up.

i. Examples of questions you might want to ask hospital patients are the following:

What has been your source of strength during your illness?

Follow up with: ———————— How is that working for you?

Follow up with: ———————— May I share with you my source of strength?

Where has God been during your time of illness?

Follow up with: ———————— Do you know that God said that He would never leave you?

How long have you been in the hospital?

Follow up with: ———————— How has it been going?

      j.   Questions you might want to ask those on an airplane, bus, subway, or train:

What is your destination today?

Follow up with: ———————— What is your final destination?

They usually look a little bewildered. Ask them again and then tell them you are asking them what will be their destination when they die. Follow up their answer with: I know where I am going and you can have that same assurance. Would you like to talk about it?

      k.   Write your own gospel tract. Keep it at about 500 words. Design a cover that reveals who you are. We are all famous for something. Maybe it is the cookies or pies you make. If this is you, design a picture of your favorite pie or cookies as your cover for your tract. You should have three main points in your tract. Write your testimony. Tell what your life was like BEFORE you accepted Jesus as your Savior. Then write about the circumstances, including WHEN and WHERE you accepted Jesus. How did you feel? Finally, write about the CHANGES that took place AFTER committing your life to Jesus. It is always good to end with a scripture and a short prayer of salvation. My personal tract has a picture of me holding a large syringe with the needle attached.

I have had the privilege of speaking many times at the following organizations. They each conduct conferences with excellent speakers. Hospital Christian Fellowship also publishes a quarterly magazine for $20.00 a year.

1. The Medical Strategic Network – P.O. Box 2052 Redlands, Ca. 92373 (866-295-METS) www.GoMETS.org and fireseeds@ GoMETS.org
2. Hospital Christian Fellowship – P.O. Box 4004 San Clemente, Ca. 92674 (949-496-7655) FAX (949-496-8465) www.HCFUSA.Com E-mail: HCFUSA@gmail.com
3. Nurses for Christ – 201 West Maxwell St., Lakeland, Fla. 33803 (863–688–2541) nur4christ@hotmail.com

CHAPTER 26
YOU CAN DO IT

In the book of Acts (chapter 1, verse 8), Jesus tells us that we will be His witnesses. Jesus would not tell us to do something without His help. He equips us for every witnessing opportunity. Just trust Him. Once you become a Christian and you receive Jesus into your life, your identity is hidden in Christ. Your identity in Christ must be at the forefront of every thought. First I am a Christian, cleverly disguised as a nurse.

We are all in the health profession. As Christians, we work in the spiritual realm. The church is the hospital where the sick need to go. When witnessing to my neighbors, I ask them the following question: "Do you know where sinners go?" The usual response is, "Everyone knows that. You are going to tell me that they go to hell." "My friend, sinners go to church." Stunned by my question and answer, the Holy Spirit prepares their heart for a willingness to hear the gospel.

We need to meet people where they are in life. Without Christ, they are lost. Yes, the church is where sinners go. Praise be to God that we are forgiven. Forgiven sinners have the confidence in knowing that when they take their last breath here on earth, it will be their first breath in heaven with Jesus.

If you declare with your mouth, "Jesus Is Lord," and believe in your heart that God raised Him from the dead, you will be saved. For it is with your heart that you believe and are justified, and it is with your mouth that you profess your faith and are saved. As Scripture says, "Anyone who believes in Him will never be put to shame." For there is no difference between Jew and Gentile—the same Lord is Lord of all and richly blesses all who call on Him, for, "Everyone who calls on the name of the Lord will be saved."

How, then, can they call on the one they have not believed in? And how can they believe in the one of whom they have not heard? And how can they hear without someone preaching to them? And how can anyone preach unless they are sent? As it is written: "How beautiful are the feet of those who bring good news!

Romans 10:9-15

How beautiful are your feet? It is never too late for a heavenly pedicure. Let's get rid of the calluses and bunions from years of having our feet squeezed into shoes of doubt. God is able to do exceedingly, and abundantly above all that we could ever imagine. He is just looking for willing servants to preach the good news. You can do it. YES, YOU CAN DO IT.

CAN I GET A WITNESS?

Remember, if God can use me, He can use you.

Too many years of my Christian life have been wasted in silent testimony. I was afraid to open my mouth and be a witness for my Savior Jesus Christ. Fear, doubt, and rejection held me captive.

Does this sound familiar? If you have ever struggled with being a witness for God, then this book is for you. Be encouraged as you read how the Lord patiently held my hand, walking me through step by step in His school of obedience.

If you are willing to be a witness to others of what the Lord has done in your life, I promise you joy unspeakable in your encounters. There is no greater reward in this life than to see someone come face to face with the King of kings and the Lord of lords.

Nurse Georgee

Georgia Cohen, AKA Nurse Georgee, is the wife of Bill Cohen, mother to Scott, Ginger, and Colette; and second mother to their husbands Bill and Chris. She is the proud grandmother to Joshua, Declan, and her furry ones; Jaxon, Kalua, Bart, Hunter, and Freckles. After receiving her RN license, Georgia served our country as a 1st Lieutenant in the U. S. Army Nurse Corp. As a registered nurse, Georgia has worked in many medical arenas, with her last fourteen years of nursing in the coronary care unit. After retiring from nursing, her love for people led her to serve on a church staff as a pastor for seven years, ministering to women and the golden-agers. In her spare time, Georgia has conducted evangelism seminars, made guest appearances on Cornerstone TV, participated in radio interviews, and traveled extensively, speaking at conferences locally, across our nation, and abroad. Georgia serves as a faculty member of METS (medical evangelism training strategies). METS conducts training nationally and internationally. *Nurge Georgee* is her first book.

For speaking engagements send requests to
nursegeorgee@aol.com

Books can be purchased at Xulon Press, Amazon (Kindle), Barnes & Noble (Nook) and Google Preview.

CPSIA information can be obtained at www.ICGtesting.com
Printed in the USA
BVOW04s0940240414

351525BV00001B/1/P

9 781626 977808